ROXANA NASTASE

ENGLISH GRAMMAR PRACTICE EXPLANATIONS & EXERCISES WITH ANSWERS

SCARLET LEAF

2017

ENGLISH GRAMMAR PRACTICE

ENGLISH GRAMMAR PRACTICE

SCARLET LEAF PUBLISHING HOUSE
TORONTO
ONTARIO
CANADA
COPYRIGHT BY ROXANA NASTASE
ISBN: 978-1-988397-23-8

All rights reserved. No part of this book can be used or reproduced in any manner whatsoever without written permission, except in the case of brief quotations embodied in critical articles and reviews.

For information address Scarlet Leaf Publishing House
Scarletleafpublishinghouse@gmail.com

Available on Kindle and other retail outlets

ENGLISH GRAMMAR PRACTICE

ENGLISH GRAMMAR PRACTICE

TABLE OF CONTENTS

UNIT 1: PRESENT TENSE — 9

SIMPLE PRESENT TENSE AND PRESENT CONTINUOUS — 9

SIMPLE PRESENT TENSE — 9

PRESENT CONTINUOUS TENSE — 16

UNIT 2: PRACTICE PRESENT TENSE AND PRESENT CONTINUOUS TENSE — 28

UNIT 3: PRACTICE PRESENT TENSE – 2 — 37

UNIT 4: PROGRESSIVE TEST — 49

UNIT 5: PAST TENSES — 57

SIMPLE PAST TENSE — 57

USED TO + BARE INFINITIVE / WOULD TO + BARE INFINITIVE — 66

PAST CONTINUOUS — 68

PAST PERFECT — 71

PAST PERFECT CONTINUOUS — 75

UNIT 6: PRACTICE PAST TENSES - 1 — 77

UNIT 7: PRACTICE PAST TENSES - 2 — 86

UNIT 8: CONSOLIDATION PAST TENSE — 99

UNIT 9: PRESENT PERFECT TENSE AND PRESENT PERFECT CONTINUOUS — 107

ENGLISH GRAMMAR PRACTICE
PRESENT PERFECT TENSE   107

PRESENT PERFECT CONTINUOUS   113

UNIT 10: PRACTICE PRESENT PERFECT – 1   116

UNIT 11: PRACTICE PRESENT PERFECT – 2   123

UNIT 12: PROGRESS TEST   135

UNIT 13: FUTURE   146

SIMPLE FUTURE   146
TO BE GOING TO (NEAR FUTURE)   148
FUTURE CONTINUOUS   150
FUTURE PERFECT   151
FUTURE IN THE PAST   151

UNIT 14: PRACTICE FUTURE - 1   153

UNIT 15: PRACTICE FUTURE – 2   163

UNIT 16: FUTURE – PROGRESS TEST   170

UNIT 17: CONDITIONAL TYPE 1, 2 AND 3 AND WISHES   177

CONDITIONAL SENTENCES   177
CONDITIONAL TYPE 1   177
CONDITIONAL TYPE 2   178
CONDITIONAL TYPE 3   179
MODAL VERBS IN CONDITIONAL   179
WISHES   180

UNIT 18: PRACTICE CONDITIONAL TYPE 1 AND 2   182

ENGLISH GRAMMAR PRACTICE

UNIT 19: PRACTICE CONDITIONAL TYPE 2 AND 3	187
UNIT 20: PRACTICE WISHES	192
UNIT 21: CONDITIONALS AND WISHES CONSOLIDATION	197
UNIT 22: MODAL VERBS	202
MODAL VERBS IN PRESENT	202
MODAL VERBS IN THE PAST	205
UNIT 23: PRACTICE MODAL VERBS	206
UNIT 24: PASSIVE VOICE	210
UNIT 25: PRACTICE PASSIVE VOICE	214
UNIT 26: REPORTED SPEECH	219
UNIT 27: PRACTICE REPORTED SPEECH	223
SOLUTION OF THE EXERCISES	230
UNIT 2: PRACTICE PRESENT TENSE AND PRESENT CONTINUOUS TENSE	230
UNIT 3: PRACTICE PRESENT TENSE – 2	235
UNIT 4: PROGRESSIVE TEST	243
UNIT 6: PRACTICE PAST TENSES - 1	248
UNIT 7: PRACTICE PAST TENSES - 2	256
UNIT 8: CONSOLIDATION PAST TENSE	266
UNIT 10: PRACTICE PRESENT PERFECT – 1	274
UNIT 11: PRACTICE PRESENT PERFECT – 2	280
UNIT 12: PROGRESS TEST	288
UNIT 14: PRACTICE FUTURE - 1	296

ENGLISH GRAMMAR PRACTICE

UNIT 15: PRACTICE FUTURE - 2	303
UNIT 16: FUTURE – PROGRESS TEST	308
UNIT 18: PRACTICE CONDITIONAL TYPE 1 AND 2	313
UNIT 19: PRACTICE CONDITIONAL TYPE 2 AND 3	318
UNIT 20: PRACTICE WISHES	323
UNIT 21: CONDITIONALS AND WISHES CONSOLIDATION	327
UNIT 23: PRACTICE MODAL VERBS	332
UNIT 25: PRACTICE PASSIVE VOICE	336
UNIT 27: PRACTICE REPORTED SPEECH	340

ENGLISH GRAMMAR PRACTICE

UNIT 1: PRESENT TENSE

SIMPLE PRESENT TENSE AND PRESENT CONTINUOUS

EXPLANATIONS

A.   Situations:

SIMPLE PRESENT TENSE

1. *To express a generally valid truth*
    Ex: Earth goes round the Sun.

2. *To show that a certain present action develops repeatedly or frequently*
    Ex: I often go with them to the sea.

Note: *Generally, an adverb or an adverbial phrase is present in the sentence in such a situation: always, often, rarely, every day, twice a month etc.*

Exception: *if we want to express irritation, annoyance or a negative emotion, then, although the action presents a certain frequency, the verb is in present continuous to emphasize the respective affirmation.*

ENGLISH GRAMMAR PRACTICE

Ex: You are always breaking something while washing up!

3. There are certain verbs used only in Simple Present Tense

to know	to own	to seem	to want
to understand	to agree	to love	to smell
to mean	to hate	to see	to wish
to belong	to like	to hear	to believe
to hope	to need	to sound	to have
to realise	to appear	to taste	to recognize

Exceptions:

TO HAVE - *when it is used in phrases, it changes its meaning and therefore, may be used in Simple or Continuous Present Tense, up to the situation*

Ex1: I have dinner at six o'clock in the evening. (habitual action)

Ex2: I'm having dinner at six o'clock in the evening. (action taking place only this evening)

TO SMELL - *when it is followed by a direct object may be used in Simple Present Tense or Continuous Tense up to the situation.*

Ex1: He is smelling a rose.
Ex2: He smells the roses in the garden every day.

TO SEE - *when its meaning is TO MEET may be used in Simple Present Tense or Continuous Tense up to the situation.*

ENGLISH GRAMMAR PRACTICE

Ex. 1: She sees him every day. (Simple Present – frequency)

Ex. 2: She is seeing him at three o'clock today. (Present Continuous, temporary action)

➔ when it is used in forming expressions - it changes meaning

Ex.: to see off ➔ may be used in Simple Present Tense or in Continuous Tense up to the situation.

TO TASTE - *in situations like:*

a) *To show that something is tasteful ➔ then, we use Simple Present Tense*

Ex.: This soup tastes great!

b) *To show that someone wants to see if there is necessary to put something into a dish or to let it as it is, then, we can use the verb either in Simple Present Tense or in Present Continuous, depending on the situation.*

Ex.1: I always taste the soup to see if it is salty enough.
Ex.2: What are you doing? – I'm tasting the soup.

ENGLISH GRAMMAR PRACTICE

TO HEAR - *in situations like:*

    a) *To show the perception of hearing* ➔ *Simple Present Tense*

        Ex.1: What's that? I hear a noise.

    b) *To show a situation similar to listening:*

➔ *Simple Present Tense if we have a truth or a frequency*

    Ex.: Judges hear people during trials.

➔ *Present Continuous if we have a temporary situation*

    Ex.: What's the judge doing? - The judge is hearing the witness now.

TO HATE / TO LOVE – *used in Present Continuous Tense only to show a temporary action*

    Ex.: I'm hating this book!

to think ➔ *1. to believe (showing opinion)* ➔ *Simple Present Tense*

    Ex: I think you're right.

    ➔ *2. actual action of thinking* ➔ *Simple Present Tense / Present Continuous Tense*

    Ex. 1: I always think of you, you know that.
    Ex. 2: I'm thinking of you right now.

to expect ➔ *1. related to expectations*

    Ex.: I expect it will clear up.

    ➔ *2. when you wait for someone or something*

ENGLISH GRAMMAR PRACTICE

Ex.: I'm expecting some friends

TO BE may be used in Present Continuous Tense only when we want to emphasize the negative behaviour of someone in a certain moment.
Note the difference:

Ex.1: He is a very naughty boy. (*general feature*)
Ex.2: He is being very naughty today. (*temporary situation*)

4. When the verbs express a non-durative action, the verb is used in Simple Present Tense.

Ex.: The boy suddenly jumps in the middle of the room.

5. When we express habits or features:

Ex1: They have dinner at seven o'clock in the evening. (habit)

Ex2: They are having dinner at seven o'clock this evening. (temporary action)

6. Simple Present Tense is used to present a demonstration, to comment a match, to give instructions

Ex: The boy takes the ball and passes it to his colleague. This one runs to the other side of the field and scores.

7. The Simple Present Tense is also used to tell a story in present even if the action took place in the past or to make a statement.

Ex: I bet you read a novel and you don't learn.

8. We use Simple Present Tense for:

→ *titles for articles in newspapers and magazine*
Ex: Factory blows up in the north.

→ *instructions; itineraries*
Ex: You take the flour and the butter and rub them together.

→ *calendar references*
Ex: In April, I go to Brasov; in June, I go to Arad.

→ *in scenarios for instructions*
Ex: The actor gets onto the stage on the right side of the stage. He walks to the middle of the stage.

9. *We may use a verb in Simple Present Tense to express a future, when the action is formally planned or to refer to timetables for trains, planes, buses and so on.*

Ex: The conference starts at ten o'clock tomorrow.

10. *Present Simple Tense shows the simultaneity of the action in a clause sentence with the action in the main sentence whose verb is in the future.*

Ex: The boy will leave when we get there.

11. We use it in conditional sentences when the verb in the main sentence is in the future.

Ex: He will come if you call him up.

ENGLISH GRAMMAR PRACTICE

PRESENT CONTINUOUS TENSE

1. When the action takes place in the moment of speaking, the verb may
be in Present Continuous.

    Ex: I'm reading a book (now).

2. When the action takes place in the future and is informally planned, we
may use Present Continuous Tense.

    Ex: Next year, we are going to the sea.

3. When we want to show an action in progression, we use Present Continuous.

    Ex: It is getting colder every day.

ENGLISH GRAMMAR PRACTICE

B. CONJUGATION OF VERBS

SIMPLE PRESENT TENSE

1.1. Affirmative

1.1.1. Generally, we use the bare infinitive for all the persons, but the third
person singular (he. she, it) where we add -s to the bare infinitive.

To-infinitive: ex: to live
Bare infinitive: ex: live

I want	we want
you want	you want
he wants	they want

1.1.2. When the verb ends in –o, we use the bare infinitive
for all the persons, but the third person of the singular,
where we add –es.

Ex: to go
I go	We go
You go	You go
He go**es**	They go

ENGLISH GRAMMAR PRACTICE

1.1.3. When the verb ends in **-x**, **-ss**, **-ch**, **-sh**, **-z**, we use the bare infinitive for all persons, but for the third person singular where we add **-es** (pronounced **i:z**)

Ex: to touch

I touch	We touch
You touch	You touch
He touch**es**	They touch

1.1.4. When the verb ends in **-y**, we use the bare infinitive for all the persons, but for the third person of the singular, where:

1.1.4.1. We add **-s**, if there is a vowel before **y**
Ex: to buy, to stay, to pay, etc.
He buy**s**; He stay**s**; He pay**s**

1.1.4.2. When there is a consonant before **-y**, for the third person singular **y** changes into **-i+es** (pronounced **i:z**)
Ex: to study

I study	We study
You study	You study
He stud**ies**	They study

EXCEPTION: TO SAY, at the third person singular adds directly **-S** but
changes the pronunciation
Ex.: He say**s** (**se:z**)

The verbs TO BE, TO HAVE and MODAL VERBS have their own conjugation:

TO BE: I am; you are; he is; she is; it is; we are; you are; they are
- short forms: I'm; you're; he's; she's; it's; we're; you're; they're.

TO HAVE: I have; you have; he has; she has; it has; we have; you have;
they have. ;
- short forms: I've, you've, he's, she's it's, we've, you've, they've

OBSERVATION: The British people prefer to use TO HAVE GOT (conjugating TO HAVE and adding the participle of TO GET) instead of TO HAVE to express possession:

I've got	it's got
you've got	we've got
he's got	you've got
she's got	they've got

Modal verbs do not add anything to the third person singular.
Ex: he can

1.2. Negative

*For Simple Present negative we use **the auxiliary TO DO**. We do not use it for the verbs TO BE and the Modal Verbs, which form the negative form with no help. TO HAVE GOT forms the negative without any auxiliary, because TO HAVE is the auxiliary.*

Negative form:

subject + do not + bare infinitive (for all persons excepting the third person singular)

Ex: I do not go there every week.

Or the short form:

subject + don't + bare inf.

Ex: I don't go there every week.

For the third person singular:

subject + does not + bare inf.

Ex: He does not have lunch at one o'clock every day.

Or the short form

subject+ doesn't + bare inf.

Ex: He doesn't have lunch at one o'clock every day.

TO BE - negative form:

I am not	She is not
You are not	It is not
He is not	We are not

You are not	They are not

Or the short forms:

I'm not	We're not / We aren't
You're not / You aren't	You're not / You aren't
He's not / He isn't	They're not / They aren't
She's not / She isn't	
It's not / It isn't	

For modal verbs, "not" is added directly to the verb, and in most situations in short form:

    Ex: I cannot / I can't

    Ex: He cannot / He can't

TO HAVE GOT

I haven't got	We haven't got
You haven't got	You haven't got
He hasn't got	They haven't got

1.3. Interrogative

All verbs, excepting the verbs TO BE, TO HAVE GOT and Modal Verbs, form the interrogative with the auxiliary TO DO:

    - for all person, excepting the third person singular:

        Do + subject + bare inf. ?

    Ex: Do you go to mountain every week?

    - for the third person singular

        Does + subject + bare inf.?

    Ex: Does he read a novel twice a week?

For TO BE:

Am I?	Is it?
Are you?	Are we?
Is he?	Are you?
Is she?	Are they?

For TO HAVE GOT:

Have I got?	Has it got?
Have you got?	Have we got?
Has he got?	Have you got?
Has she got?	Has it got?

For Modal Verbs: Modal verb + subject?

Ex: Can you come? ; Must she go there?

1.4. Interrogative -Negative

All verbs, excepting the verbs TO BE, TO HAVE GOT and Modal Verbs, form the interrogative with the auxiliary TO DO:

For all persons excepting the third person singular:

Do + subject + not + bare inf.?

Don't + subject + bare inf.? *(for short forms)*

Ex: Do you not like the soup? / Don't you like the soup?

For the third person singular:

Does + subject + not + bare inf.?

Doesn't + subject + bare inf.? *(for short forms)*

Ex: Does he not go to the mountains every summer?

Doesn't he go to the mountains every summer?

For TO BE:

Am I not?	Are we not?
Are you not?	Are you not?
Is he not?	Are they not?

Short forms:

Aren't you?	Aren't you?
Isn't he?	Aren't they?
Aren't we?	

TO HAVE GOT

Ex: Have you not got? / Haven't you got? (*short form*)

MODAL VERBS

Ex: Can't you leave it like that?
Can't he come tomorrow?

NOTE: *Generally, in spoken language, the short forms are preferred*

PRESENT CONTINUOUS TENSE

NOTE: To express the continuous aspect of all tenses (present, past, future), we use the auxiliary TO BE at the respective tense and we add -ING to the bare infinitive of the verb.

Therefore, for present tense:

2.1. Affirmative

> **subject + to be (pres.) + [vb.+-ing]**

> Ex: He's reading a book.
> I'm just having lunch.
> They're doing their homework.
> We're listening to some music and having fun.
> You're wasting your time with that book.

2.2. Negative

> **subject + to be (pres. neg.) + [vb.+-ing]**

> Ex: He isn't reading a book.
> I'm not looking for anything.
> We aren't going to the theatre tonight.
> You aren't listening to me.
> They aren't watching movies.

2.3. Interrogative

to be (pres.) + subject + [vb. + -ing]?

Ex: Is he reading that book?

Are you leaving now?

2.4. Interrogative-Negative

to be (pres.) + subject + not + [vb. + - ing]?

Ex: Is he not going there?

Are we not going to Charles this evening?

Are they not coming to us tomorrow?

Or with the short form of the verb TO BE negative:

to be (pres. neg.) + subject + [vb. + - ing]?

Ex: Isn't he going there with them?

Aren't you doing your homework?

[VERB + -ING]

It represents:

- gerund
- present participle
- the mark of the present continuous

ENGLISH GRAMMAR PRACTICE

Formation:

1. Generally, by adding directly **ING** to the bare infinitive of the verb

    ex: read+- **ING** → reading

2. To the verbs ending in **-e**, we remove **-e** before putting **-ING**

    ex: live+- **ING** → living

    Exception: see → seeing; be → being

3. When verbs end in **-ie**, **-ie** turns into **-Y** and then we add **ING**.

    ex: lie+- **ING** → lying

4. When verbs end in **-el**, we double **-l** (only in British English) before **-ING**, as well as in the case of the verbs ending in **–er**, where **–r** is doubled before **-ING**.

    ex: travel + - **ING** → travelling
           refer + - **ING** → referring

5. When short verbs have a vowel between two consonants or between a semi- vowel and a consonant, we double the last consonant before **-ing**:

    ex:

put → putting	stop → stopping
let → letting	shop → shopping
get → getting	cut → cutting
sit → sitting	drop → dropping

shut ➔ shutting   begin ➔ beginning
swim ➔ swimming

But attention!!!

Sing ➔ singing
Think ➔ thinking
Drink ➔ drinking

UNIT 2: PRACTICE PRESENT TENSE AND PRESENT CONTINUOUS TENSE

1. *Write the **-s/-es** forms of these verbs:*

   go;   live;   write;   answer;   touch;
   miss;   do;   read;   study;   play;   enter;

2. *This is what Mark does every day:*

Mark is a mail carrier. He wakes up at six o'clock in the morning. He goes to the bathroom and washes himself. Then he gets dressed, goes into the kitchen and has breakfast. He usually drinks tea and eats a sandwich for his breakfast. Then he washes the dishes and leaves for the post-office. There he takes the letters and newspapers he must deliver and leaves the post-office. He delivers the letters and the newspapers and then comes back to the post-office. He finishes work at five o'clock in the afternoon and goes back home. He arrives at home at six and has a snack. He reads a book or watches TV until eight o'clock. Then he has dinner. After dinner, he takes a shower and then goes to bed.

a) *Find the examples of the Present Simple.*

b) *Compare your situation and Mark's situation.*

c) Write about your best friend. What does he or she do every day?

3. Complete the sentences. Use the words: **do, does, don't, doesn't, go, goes**:

a) _____ he _____ to school every day? - No, he sometimes _____ to the stadium.
b) I _____ to the theatre twice a month. _____ you _____ to the theatre too? - Yes, I _____, but I _____ only once a month.
c) _____ they _____ to their aunt's house in the country every summer? – No, they_____, only Keith _____ .

4. Ask questions using the words below and present tense simple; add **do, does**:

a) you / learn well?

b) John/sleep/in the afternoon?

c) they / come / to the sea / every year?

d) she/ drive / to office / every morning?

e) your grandmother / feel/well/usually?

ENGLISH GRAMMAR PRACTICE

5. Write the *-ING* forms of these words:

go, touch, die, quarrel, put, ask, drop, lie, study, see, write

6. Use the words to write sentences or questions (use either present simple tense or present tense continuous for the verbs):

a) you / live / with / your friends / these days

b) they / come / to the cinema / with us / this afternoon

c) Liz / not read / in her room / now

d) they / drive / to the sea / this week

e) we / not learn / for the exam / today

f) John / go / to the circus / now?

g) Joshua and Ann / eat / their lunch / at the moment?

h) you / not come / with them / to the show?

i) he / write / the letter / right now?

j) We / spend / time / with friends / every Sunday

7. Complete the following sentences. Use the Present Continuous or Present Simple for the verbs given:

(a) drive, get up, drink, dress, have

He .... at nine o'clock every day but today he ....at seven. He usually .... tea at breakfast but today he .... coffee. He....................... in a suit for work every morning but today it is Saturday and he .... casual clothes. He .... to the sea with Tom in his car now.

(b) spend, work, teach, not pay

John is a history teacher. He .... a lot of time at school every day. Today he .... five hours. He .... the history of the world. He ....Ancient History today. He is upset because the children .... attention in class now.

ENGLISH GRAMMAR PRACTICE

8. Complete the questions. Use the Present Continuous or Present Simple.

a) they / sometimes / come / to you?

b) you / go / with them / to church today?

c) it / get / warmer / every day?

d) we / drive / to office / this morning?

e) he / write / a novel / these days?

f) she / knit / a pullover / for her sister?

g) you / live / with your grandparents / this week?

h) she / sleep / at the house?

i) they / usually / learn / in the morning?

j) he / never / do / his homework?

9. Complete the sentences. Use present simple or present continuous.

a) He _____ (like) going to the swimming pool in the afternoon.

b) She _____ (taste) your cake now.

c) The food _____ (taste) better now. You have put some spices, haven't you?

d) Leonora _____ (need) a new bike. Hers is broken.

e) We _____ (own) a bigger house now.

f) The book _____ (belong) to John. It's a present from Ann.

g) I _____ (realise) that I've made a mistake.

h) She _____ (think) of her work at the moment.

i) John _____ (think) he is right and he is.

j) I _____(expect) you succeed.

   I _____ (expect) news from you after the exam.

10. *Correct the sentences, if necessary:*

   a) John and Ann are liking the food today.

   b) I'm thinking of my holiday now.

   c) We are going to school in the mornings.

   d) They are living with their friends this year.

   e) She is swimming quite well.

   f) It is smelling good in the kitchen. They've made a cake.

   g) The rose smells good. I'm loving it.

   h) I'm seeing Alice across the street.

   i) They're agreeing with you in this matter.

   j) I like to dress casually.

ENGLISH GRAMMAR PRACTICE

11. Add **am**, **are**, **is**, **have** or **has** to complete the following sentences:

a) I _____ ready to go with you to school.

b) They _____ a new job in the other town.

c) Joshua _____ going to Glasgow next week.

d) She _____ a new sports car.

e) You _____ my best friend.

f) They _____ leaving this afternoon.

g) Robert _____ a good swimmer, indeed.

h) They _____ not what we imagined. They _____ only freshmen.

i) You don't _____ any right to come here and say that.

j) She _____ not leaving now. She _____ staying some more time.

12. *Choose the correct word or phrase underlined:*

a) Ann goes / is going to the circus this evening.

b) They listen / are listening to the news every day.

c) It rains / is raining. I've taken my umbrella.

d) Lucy and Dan live / are living in a house near the sea.

e) They don't go / aren't going to Paris next year.

f) We spend / are spending a lot of time in the library. We study / are
a) studying a lot.

g) I look / am looking for a book on this subject.

h) Mary has a new job. She works / is working in a hospital.

i) The children are / are being naughty today. They don't listen / aren't listening to anything they're told.

j) You write / are writing nice letters.

UNIT 3: PRACTICE PRESENT TENSE – 2

1. For each situation, decide which expressions are possible in the context given:

a) You are in the classroom and you don't know what your colleagues are talking about. You ask a colleague nearby:
    1. Do you know what is about?
    2. Please, tell me what is about. Do you know?
    3. Do you know what is about? Tell me!

b) You are in the street and you don't know the direction to the post-office. You ask a passerby:
    1. Do you know where the post-office is? Tell me!
    2. Do you mind if I ask you where the post-office is?
    3. Could you tell me where the post-office is?

c) You are in a shop with a friend. You want to buy a dress but you can't make up your mind. You ask your friend:
    1. Which one you think I should buy?
    2. Can you tell me which fits me best?
    3. What do you think? Which I am going to buy?

d) You want to rent a flat but you don't know any. You ask a friend:
   1. I want to rent a flat. Do you know any?
   2. What do you think? Can you tell me where to move?
   3. Do you mind telling me where to move?

e) You need a book from a friend to write an essay. You say:
   1. I need a book. Give it to me!
   2. You don't need the book, but I do. Give it to me!
   3. Could you lend me this book? I need it, please.

f) You are visiting a friend in hospital. You ask him:
   1. How do you feel? Is it better?
   2. Can you tell me how do you feel?
   3. What do you think? Is it better?

g) You meet an old friend in the street and find out he has a new job. You ask:
   1. How do you go on? Is it all right?
   2. Do you go on with your new job?
   3. What do you think? Is it better?

h) You want to visit a friend and you call him. You say:
   1. I want to come to you. You don't mind.
   2. What do you think? May I come to you?
   3. I want to visit you. Are you home?

ENGLISH GRAMMAR PRACTICE

i) You need a new coat. You tell your mother:
   1. I need a new coat. Buy it!
   2. Can you buy me a new coat? I need one.
   3. Do you think you could possibly buy me a new coat?

j) You want to invite a friend to the swimming pool. You say:
   1. I'm going to the swimming pool. You come with me.
   2. I'm going to the swimming pool. Do you think you could possibly come too?
   3. I'm going to the swimming pool. Could you come too?

2. Decide if the following sentences are possible:

   a) I'm going to the match tomorrow.
   b) He is liking ice cream.
   c) They are coming to you every day now.
   d) She is feeling well today.
   e) I need a new book from the bookshop.
   f) She is leaving for Miami every summer.
   g) We are going to the movie this evening.
   h) I'm hating this book!
   i) Alan wants to go with you.
   j) They are realising they have made a mistake.

3. Choose the correct phrases underlined in each sentence:

a) Noreen <u>is going</u> / <u>goes</u> to the mountain with the Browns next week.

b) What <u>is this action involving</u> / <u>does this action involve</u>?

c) I <u>am meaning</u> / <u>mean</u> it. I'm going to get very angry.

d) Susan <u>is leaving</u> / <u>leaves</u> with them.

e) George <u>is always going</u> / <u>always goes</u> to the movies on Saturday.

f) He <u>is always breaking</u> / <u>always breaks</u> something while washing dishes.

g) Neil <u>is coming</u> / <u>comes</u> to visit you twice a year.

h) I <u>am preferring</u> / <u>prefer</u> tea.

i) She <u>is needing</u> / <u>needs</u> a new bag.

j) I <u>am recognizing</u> / <u>recognize</u> her now. She's Ann's niece.

ENGLISH GRAMMAR PRACTICE

4. Read the answers and then complete the questions:

a) _____? Lucy? No, she's not coming to us this afternoon.

b) _____? The castle? Yes, we're going to the castle.

c) _____? Spanish? No, I don't. I learn German.

d) _____? Here? Yes, I think she's here now.

e) _____? This spring? No, we are painting the house this summer.

f) _____? TV? No, we don't. We prefer listening to music.

g) _____? Geography? Yes, they study geography at school.

h) _____? No, I'm sorry, but you may not smoke here.

i) _____? Yes, they have. They've got a big dog.

ENGLISH GRAMMAR PRACTICE

j) _____? No, she's not buying a car. She doesn't know to drive.

5. Rewrite each sentence so that the verb is a negative contraction:

a) I'm going to the museum this afternoon.
b) She lives in a house near the school.
c) They come to us once a month.
d) Ann and George are going to the show this evening.
e) He is having lunch at the moment.
f) She is doing her homework in her room.
g) The boys drive to college every morning.
h) Ann and John watch TV in the evening.
i) We are building a new house this summer.
j) She is staying with her brother for the moment.

6. Complete each sentence with a present simple form or a present continuous form, using the words given:

a) Laura _____ with her family in the suburbs. (live)
b) They _____ in the park in the afternoons. (play)
c) We _____ any new clothes this season. (not need)
d) They _____ their friends in the disco this evening (see)
e) She _____ her homework on time. (never, do)

f) The children _____ with their parents to the circus on Sunday. (go)

g) She and I _____ each other these days. (see)

h) We _____ the committee. (ever, misinform)

i) You _____ enough and that is why you are so tired. (not rest)

j) I _____ him any letter. (not send)

7. Choose the correct spelling form for each pair of words:

writeing/writing   liveing/living
seeing/seing   quarreling/quarrelling
droping/dropping   eatting/eating
being/bing   studying/studing

8. *Put each sentence in the form requires:*

a) She is reading a novel now. (negative)
b) They don't live in the country. (interrogative-negative)
c) She isn't coming to school today. (affirmative)
d) The boy does his homework every day. (negative)
e) He is riding his bike in the neighbourhood at the hour. (question)
f) We are giving them a phone call at the moment. (negative)
g) I am not leaving to the theatre now. (affirmative)
h) He works in an office in the harbour. (negative)
i) They go skating every winter. (negative)
j) You are coming at six. (question)

ENGLISH GRAMMAR PRACTICE

9. *Choose the correct word or phrase underlined:*

a) Joshua <u>usually</u> / <u>all the time</u> goes to school on the bus.
b) They are going to the doctor <u>in the afternoons</u> / <u>in the afternoon</u>.
c) She is listening to the news <u>recently</u> / <u>at the moment</u>.
d) This boy <u>normally</u> / <u>continuously</u> lives with his grandparents.
e) Susie is <u>always</u> / <u>lately</u> coming late to school.
f) George doesn't <u>ever</u> / <u>never</u> read a book.
g) Lucia and Ann read a lot <u>recently</u> / <u>normally</u>.
h) I am very attentive in class <u>now</u> / <u>recently</u>.
i) She is buying a new car <u>nowadays</u> / <u>at the moment</u>.
j) We <u>usually</u> / <u>forever</u> have four classes a day.

10. Put each verb given into present simple or present continuous:

a) They usually _____ (drive) to office in the morning.
b) She never _____ (stay) late in town.
c) He _____ (come) with us to the sea this summer.
d) Josh _____ (not want) to go with them to the theatre this evening.
e) We _____ (look for) that book in the bookcase for the moment.
f) She _____ (always, leave) her clothes all over the floor!
g) Tom _____ (think) of breaking up with Mary because he's very upset.
h) The child is hungry. It _____ (eat) everything.
i) Mrs. Smith _____ (cook) dinner because people _____ (come) to dinner. She _____ (usually, cook) very well.
j) Mary _____ (cry) in her room because she's lost her favourite ribbon.

ENGLISH GRAMMAR PRACTICE

11. Choose the best continuation of the conversation by joining the appropriate sentences in the two columns:

a) Are you coming to me this evening?

b) What are you doing at the moment?

c) They are going on a trip next week. What are you saying?

d) She is going to the doctor this afternoon, I hear. What's wrong?

e) Mary and Tom are coming to visit us this evening. Are you at home?

f) You are too busy, I'm afraid.

g) Are you thinking of going to the mountains this winter?

h) Lucy says she's buying a new car and driving to Paris next month.

i) Are you playing basketball this weekend?

j) They are going to town. Do you need anything?

1. I don't know. People say she's run down at the moment.

2. I'm in France next week and I don't know when I come back.

3. Yes, I know. I have a lot of work to do and I have no spare time at all.

4. I don't think so. I don't have vacation until in the summer.

5. I'm going to Quebec this weekend.

6. She is having an important interview there.

7. I'm having a meeting at the office and I might be too late.

8. Yes, I am. I'm not working this afternoon after program.

9. I'm going shopping myself later.

10. I'm having lunch and then I'm going to bed. I'm

very tired.

12. *Put each verb given into present simple or present continuous:*

a) It _____ (rain) and you must take your umbrella.

b) It is very cold. – Yes, indeed. And the wind _____ (blow) too.

c) It _____ (smell) good in the house. – Yes, mother _____ (cook).

d) They _____ (go) shopping in town this afternoon. They _____ (always, go) shopping in the afternoon.

e) They are at the bakers. The _____ (buy) some bread and cakes for tea.

f) We _____ (go) to buy tickets for the theatre. You _____ (come) with us?

g) She _____ (like) to drink a black coffee in the morning. She _____ (drink) coffee now.

h) Ann _____ (call) me. I _____ (go) to the show with her.

i) They _____ (ride) their motorcycles every weekend.

j) You _____ (think) of going to them next week, aren't you?

ENGLISH GRAMMAR PRACTICE

UNIT 4: PROGRESSIVE TEST

1. Choose the most appropriate words underlined:

a) John likes / is liking playing football with his friends in the schoolyard every Saturday. He plays / is playing football with them this Saturday too.

b) They do / are doing their homework now. They always do / are doing their homework at this hour.

c) She never calls / is calling us. We usually call / are calling her.

d) I leave / am leaving by bus to Barrie this afternoon.

e) This car doesn't belong / isn't belonging to me.

f) They mean / are meaning they don't go / aren't going with you.

g) What do you do / are you doing this afternoon? I read / am reading for my essay.

h) She comes / is coming to me this evening. We go / are going to Susan's party.

i) Briana writes / is writing interesting compositions. She presents / is presenting one at school tomorrow.

j) Janice and Jean have / are having lunch in town tomorrow.

ENGLISH GRAMMAR PRACTICE

2. Choose the most suitable word or phrase to complete each sentence:

a) Alicia _____ for her cat.

    1. looks

    2. is looking

b) I _____ my bike behind the house in the evening.

    1. leave

    2. am leaving

c) They _____ you to succeed in this exam.

    1. expect

    2. are expecting

d) We _____ with them in this matter.

    1. agree

    2. are agreeing

e) Mary _____ guests this Sunday.

    1. expects

    2. is expecting

f) They _____ to town this afternoon.

    1. drive

    2. are driving

g) She _____ to Italy to study Italian.

    1. goes

    2. is going

h) I _____ to buy a flat in this area.

    1. want

    2. am wanting

i) She _____

ENGLISH GRAMMAR PRACTICE

   1. usually feels run down   2. is usually feeling run down

   j) He _____ I am right.
      1. thinks   2. is thinking

3. *Put each verb in brackets in the most suitable present tense:*

   a) I _____ (not feel) well and I (not know) if I _____ (can) manage today.

   b) They _____ (leave) for a short trip in the mountains this weekend.

   c) Kate's friends _____ (come) to visit her today. They _____ (usually, visit) her once a month.

   d) She _____ (have) her birthday party this Saturday and she _____ (invite) all her friends.

   e) We _____ (usually, help) our mother with the spring cleaning.

   f) They _____ (travel) with their friends every year. This year they _____ (travel) to London.

   g) I _____ (recognize) you now. You are Mary's niece, aren't you?

   h) What _____ (they, do)? They _____ (play) chess in their room and they are happy.

ENGLISH GRAMMAR PRACTICE

i) He _____ (appreciate) your work. You _____ (usually, do) a good job.

j) Hurry up! The train _____ (leave) the station.

4. Rewrite each sentence so that the meaning stays the same:

a) He is never listening to what I am telling him.
   He keeps _____
b) The beginning of the English class is at nine.
   The English class _____
c) Lauren never visits us in summer.
   Lauren doesn't _____
d) She's determined to leave the town on Sunday.
   She's _____, there's no doubt.
e) The school year finishes in June.
   The end of _____.
g) I want to go to the disco. What do you say?
   What about _____?
h) What do you have in mind? Are you going to them?
   Are you _____?
i) You have too many clothes on you.
   You are _____.
j) Which is your book?
   Which book_____?

ENGLISH GRAMMAR PRACTICE

5. Put each verb in brackets in the most suitable present tense:

a) John's daughter _____ (play) the violin very well. She _____ (play) in this concert at school.

b) _____ (go, they) to the sea this summer? They _____ (usually, go) to the sea in July.

c) We _____ (spend) our winter holiday in Quebec this year, even though we (prefer) going to Florida.

d) I _____ (enjoy) spending time with them. That is why I _____ (go) with them to the country this weekend.

e) Ann _____ (spend) too much and therefore she _____ (have) no money at the end of the month.

f) They _____ (run) this evening in the park. They _____ (want) to keep themselves in a good shape.

g) What time you _____ (get up) on Sundays? - I _____ (usually get up) at ten, but during the week I _____ (get up) at seven.

h) I _____ (go) swimming today and I _____ (think) of inviting her too.

i) I've arranged to go to Madrid. I _____ (spend) a few days there with friends.

ENGLISH GRAMMAR PRACTICE

j) What _____ (this business, involve)? _____ (I, travel) a lot?

6. Rewrite each sentence so that it contains the word in capitals and the meaning stays the same:

a) She is going to London on vacation this summer. (**SPENDING**)
b) We aren't too fond of chocolate cakes. (**LIKE**)
c) Sue and Dan are leaving for work by car this morning. (**DRIVING**)
d) He is walking to office today. (**ON FOOT**)
e) He is a good footballer. (**PLAYS**)
f) I don't mind if you go there. (**CARE**)
g) It doesn't matter if it rains today. (**IMPORTANT**)
h) How much is this shirt, please? (**COST**)
i) Mother is going shopping today. (**TO**)
j) I don't know if I want to go there. (**SURE**)

ENGLISH GRAMMAR PRACTICE

7. *Choose the most appropriate word or phrase underlined:*

   a) We don't work too much these days/currently.
   b) Georgia isn't listening to music lately/today.
   c) My brothers don't play football lately/every day.
   d) I don't always have lunch / I am not always having lunch at three.
   e) He is always boasting / boasts currently.
   f) I'm working till/by five o'clock today.
   g) He isn't coming before/by nine.
   h) You often don't come / are not often coming on time.
   i) She never knits/ever knits pullovers.
   j) Mandy and Kate don't do their job on time yet / always.

8. *Identify any possible errors in these sentences and correct them. Some of the sentences are correct.*

   a) She isn't listening to music every Sunday.
   b) We are never going camping over the weekend.
   c) She doesn't go to the cinema today.
   d) Melanie is cleaning the room this afternoon.
   e) Mandy is inviting friends at home every Sunday.
   f) You are always leaving your clothes on the floor!
   g) He keeps bothering me all the time.
   h) The cake is tasting good.

i) I'm smelling the flowers in this pot. They are smelling good.
j) Paula sleeps because she is being very tired and tomorrow she meets someone.

ENGLISH GRAMMAR PRACTICE

UNIT 5: PAST TENSES

EXPLANATIONS

SIMPLE PAST TENSE

A) Situations

1. Action takes place in the past and we know when ➜ simple past

      Ex: Last year we went to the mountain with them.

2. The action takes place in the past and the subject is deceased ➜ simple past

Note the difference:

      Ex1: Whitman wrote many poems.
      Ex2: J. K. Rolling has written many novels.

3. We are not interested in the moment when the action takes place, but in the place where it takes place ➜ simple past.

      Ex1: I have bought a dress.
      Ex2: I bought it from Harrods.

B) The conjugation of verbs

Generally, each verb with some exceptions presents three forms:

→ the first form: infinitive

Ex: to ask (to-infinitive)

ask (bare infinitive)

→ the second form: the past

Ex: asked

→ the third form: past participle

Ex: asked

In accordance with the third forms, the verbs are:

I. **Regular verbs**

II. **Irregular verbs**

I. **Regular verbs** are the verbs with the second and third form identical ending in **-ED**.

The second and the third form of these verbs are formed:

a. Generally, by adding **-ed** to the bare infinitive.

Ex: call - called - called

b. If the verb ends in **-e**, by adding only **-d** to the bare infinitive.

Ex: live - lived - lived

c. If the verb ends in **-y**, we have two situations:

→ the bare infinitive has a consonant before **-y**, then **-y** turns into **-i** and **-ed** is added to the bare infinitive.

Ex: cry - cried - cried

→ the verb has a vowel before **-y**, we add **-ed** directly after **-y**

Ex: enjoy - enjoyed - enjoyed

d. If the verb ends in **-el** or **-er**, we double **-l** and **-r** before adding **–ed** (mostly in British English)
Ex: travel - travelled -travelled

e. If the verb is short and has a vowel between two consonants or a semivowel and a consonant, we double the final consonant before **-ed**.
Ex: stop - stopped - stopped
     drop - dropped - dropped
     shop - shopped - shopped

II. Irregular verbs

a. Verbs we all three forms identical:
Ex:

cut - cut - cut	let - let - let
put - put - put	cost – cost – cost
set - set - set	shut – shut – shut
hurt - hurt -hurt	hit – hit - hit

b. Verbs with all forms identical but with different pronunciation:
Ex: read - read - read
     [rid] [red] [red]

c. Verbs with the first form and third form identical:
Ex: come - came - come
     become - became - become
     run - ran - run

d. Verbs with the second and third form identical ending in **-OUGHT** or **- AUGHT**:

Ex:

buy - bought - bought   teach - taught - taught
seek - sought - sought   think - thought - thought
bring - brought - brought   catch - caught - caught

e. Verbs with the second and third form identical ending in **-OLD**:

Ex: sell - sold - sold
      tell - told - told

f. Verbs with the second and third form identical ending in **-AID**:

Ex: pay - paid - paid

**1 make - made - made

g. Verbs with the second and third form identical ending in **-UG** or **-UNG**:

Ex: dig - dug - dug
      hang - hung - hung

h. Verbs with the second and third form ending in **-OUND**, coming from **-IND** from the first form:

Ex: bind - bound - bound
      find - found - found

i. Verbs with the second and third form ending in **-T** (generally added to the bare infinitive) (usually something disappears from the verb):

---

[1] ****Exception**

Ex:
spell - spelt - spelt
leave - left - left
smell - smelt - smelt
feel - felt - felt
dream - dreamt - dreamt
sleep - slept - slept
* [2]burn - burnt - burnt
sit - sat - sat
mean - meant - meant
get - got - got (gotten – American English)
meet - met - met

j. Verbs with the second and third form identical, ending in **- T**, this one coming from **- D** at the first form:

Ex: spend - spent - spent
build - built - built
send - sent - sent
lend - lent - lent

k. Verbs ending in **-ED** at the second and third form, this coming from **-EED** at the first form:

Ex: feed - fed - fed
breed - bred - bred
** lead - led - led

l. Verbs ending in **-ON** or **- ONE** at the second and third form, this coming from **-IN** respectively **-INE** at the first form:

Ex: win - won - won

---

[2] * The verb is also regular verb

shine - shone - shone

m. Verbs ending in **-OOD** at the second and third form:

    Ex: stand - stood - stood
            understand - understood - understood

n. Other verbs with the second and third form identical:

    Ex: strike - struck - struck

o. Verbs with the second and third form ending in **-D**:

    Ex: have - had - had
            hear - heard - heard

p. Verbs with all the forms different, ending in **–OW** at the first form, this one changing into **-EW** at the second form and in **–OWN** at the third form:

    Ex:

know – knew – known	** fly – flew – flown
grow – grew – grown	** show – showed - shown
blow – blew – blown	**draw – drew – drawn
throw – threw – thrown	

r. Verbs with all forms different, generally short verbs, which contain an **-I** between two consonants or between a semivowel and a consonants at first form; **-I** becomes **–A** at the second form and **–U** at the third form:

Ex:

sing – sang – sung	sink – sank – sunk
ring – rang – rung	**begin – began – begun
drink – drank – drunk	
swim – swam – swum	

s. Verbs with all forms different:

Ex:

write - wrote - written	give – gave – given
wear - wore - worn	choose – chose – chosen
tear - tore - torn	do – did – done
fall – fell – fallen	forgive – forgave – forgiven
drive – drove – driven	forget – forgot – forgotten
eat – ate – eaten	take – took – taken
hide – hid – hidden	speak – spoke – spoken
ride – rode – ridden	lie – lay – lain
steal – stole – stolen	be – was/were – been
go – went – gone	break – broke - broken

C. Effective Conjugation

1. Affirmative:

Subject + the 2nd form

Ex: He went there yesterday.

2. Negative:

NOTE: As for the simple present tense, to conjugate a verb in negative, interrogative and interrogative-negative, in simple past, we use the auxiliary **TO DO** for all verbs, (with the exception of the verb **TO BE** and of the **Modal Verbs**).

Subject + did + not + bare inf.

Ex: John did not go there yesterday.

Or for the short forms:

Subject + didn't + bare inf.

Ex: He didn't go there yesterday.

3. Interrogative

Did + subject + bare inf.?

Ex: Did you go there yesterday?

4. Interrogative - Negative

Did + subject + not + bare inf.?

Ex: Did you not go there yesterday?

Or the short form:

Didn't + subject + bare inf.?

Ex: Didn't you go there yesterday?

ENGLISH GRAMMAR PRACTICE

The forms of the verb TO BE:

1. Affirmative

I was	It was
You were	We were
He was	You were
She was	They were

2. Negative

I was not	It was not
You were not	We were not
He was not	You were not
She was not	They were not

Or the short forms:

I wasn't	It wasn't
You weren't	We weren't
He wasn't	You weren't
She wasn't	They weren't

3. Interrogative

Was I?	Was it?
Were you?	Were we?
Was he?	Were you?
Was she?	Were they?

4. Interrogative Negative

Was I not?	Were we not?
Were you not?	Were you not?
Was he not?	Were they not?
Was she not?	
Was it not?	

Or the short forms:

Wasn't I?	Wasn't it?
Weren't you?	Weren't we?
Wasn't he?	Weren't you?
Wasn't she?	Weren't they?

USED TO + BARE INFINITIVE / WOULD TO + BARE INFINITIVE

We can use: **used to + bare infinitive** or **would + bare infinitive** to show that an action was something usual in the past.

Differences:

 used to + bare infinitive - can be used with all type of verbs

  Ex. I used to spend winters in the mountains

  Ex. I used to like playing tennis when I was young.

would + bare infinitive - cannot be used with state verbs.

Ex. I would spend winters in the mountain. (correct)

Ex. I would like playing tennis when I was young.

(incorrect)

PAST CONTINUOUS

A) Situations

1. We use past continuous tense to express an action in the past that is continuous in a certain moment in the past

   Ex: Maria was reading at ten o'clock last night.

2. We use past continuous tense to express a continuous action in the past that is interrupted by another action in the past

   Ex: Maria was reading when the phone rang.

   Ex: I called her when she was writing her homework.

3. We use past continuous tense to express two continuous and simultaneous actions in the past

   Ex: While I was sleeping, she was reading that book.

Note: We cannot use past continuous tense to express an action referring to a narrative past

   Ex: When I was a child, I went with my parents to the mountains every year.

4. We can use past continuous to express a series of continuous situations to describe the background

   Ex: There were many people in the lobby. Some were reading newspapers, some were talking, some were watching TV and some were just sitting down in the armchairs.

B. Conjugations of the verbs

NOTE: Being a continuous tense, past tense continuous uses the auxiliary verb **TO BE** and **[vb+-ing]**. As past continuous is a past tense, **TO BE** will be in the past as well:

1. **Affirmative**

    Subject + to be (simple past) + [vb.+-ing]

    Ex: I was reading a book.

    Ex: He was reading.

    Ex: We were reading.

2. **Negative**

    Subject + to be (simple past) + not + [vb.+-ing]

    Ex: He was not reading.

    Or the short form:

    Subject + to be (simple past) + [vb. + - ing]

    Ex: I wasn't reading.

    Ex: You weren't reading.

    Ex: He wasn't reading.

3. **Interrogative**

    to be (simple past) + subject + [vb.+-ing]?

    Ex: Was he reading?

4. Interrogative - Negative
to be (simple past) + subject + not + [vb.+-ing]?

Ex: Was he not going there?

Or the short form:

to be (simple past) + subject + [vb. +-ing]?

Ex: Wasn't he going there?

NOTE: A state verb does not function in a continuous tense.

PAST PERFECT

A. Situations

We use past perfect to express an action that takes place before another action in the past, to show the anteriority of the action before the other one.

Time expressions used with past perfect:

before	until
after	by
as soon as	by the time

Observation:

Before and **after** do not necessarily require the use of past perfect because we can understand clearly from the sentence which action is the previous one. Therefore, especially in the spoken language, people prefer to use simple past tense together with **before** and **after**.

Ex1: Before she came, he had washed the dishes.
Ex2: Before she came, he washed the dishes.

Ex1: They went to the museum after they had met at the café.
Ex2: They went to the museum after they met at the café.

Certain verbs require the use of past perfect in the clause sentence when we have past tense in the main sentence

realise	Ex: I realised that I had forgotten the book at home.
think	Ex: I thought he had already left.
know	Ex: I knew she had come that morning.
be sure	Ex: I was sure that they had not learnt for the exam at all.
suspect	Ex: I suspected that he had stolen her bike.
understand	Ex: I understood that he had missed the plane.

Constructions with Past Perfect:

Scarcely + had + subject + 3rd form verb+ than + subject + simple past

Ex: Scarcely had he entered the office than everybody left.

No sooner + had + subject + 3rd form verb+ than + subject + simple past

Ex: No sooner had they come than the phone rang.

Hardly + had + subject + 3rd form verb+ when + subject + simple past

Ex: Hardly had she finished reading that lecture when her parents came home.

Subject + had + 3rd form verb + until + subject + simple past

Ex: No one had touched the food until they had come too.

It was + numeral ordinal + subject + had + 3rd form verb

Ex: It was the second cake he had eaten.

Ex: It was the sixth dress she had changed.

It was + adjective superlative + subject + had + ever + 3rd form verb

Ex: It was the most interesting film I had ever seen.

Ex: It was the most beautiful girl he had ever dated.

B. Conjugation

I. Affirmative

Subject + had + the third form of the vb.

Ex: The cat saw me *as soon as* it **had seen** me.

2. Negative

Subject + had not + the third form of the verb

Ex: *The child* **had not learnt** *anything* by the time I came home.

Subject + hadn't + the third form of the vb.

Ex: *The child* **hadn't learnt** *anything* by the time I came home.

3. Interrogative

Had + subject + the third form of the verb?

Ex: **Had you arrived** there by the time they came?

4. Interrogative - Negative

Had + subject + not + the third form of the verb?

Ex: ***Had you not arrived*** *there* by the time they came?

Hadn't + subject + the third form of the verb?

Ex: ***Hadn't you arrived*** *there* by the time they came?

PAST PERFECT CONTINUOUS

A. Situations:

1. To express an action that starts previously to another action in the past and that goes on after the action in the past takes place.

> Ex: He *was reading* at noon yesterday when we *came*. He **had been reading** all morning.

2. We may also use past perfect continuous to show the contrast between a previous action in the past and a continuous action, which is also previous to that moment in the past.

B. Conjugation

NOTE: Being the continuous aspect of a tense we have to use the verb **TO BE** and *[vb.+-ING]*; being past perfect, we use **TO BE** in the past perfect

1. Affirmative
subject + had + been + [vb.+ -ing]
Ex: He had been reading.

2. Negative
subject + hadn't + been + [vb.+ -ing]
Ex: He hadn't been reading.

3. Interrogative

Had + subject + been + [vb.+ -ing]?

Ex: Had he been reading?

4. Interrogative - Negative

Had + subject + been + [vb.+ -ing]?

Ex: Hadn't he been reading?

UNIT 6: PRACTICE PAST TENSES - 1

1. *What were the first jobs of these people? Complete the sentences. Use **is**, **am**, **are**, **was**, **were**:*

   a) John _____ a bank director now, but he _____ a clerk bank last year.

   b) They _____ teachers now, but last year, they _____ office-workers.

   c) She _____ an optician now, but three years ago, she _____ a nurse.

   d) We _____ librarians now, but last year, we _____ salesmen.

   e) I _____ a writer now, but two years ago, I _____ a journalist.

   f) You _____ an engineer now, but a few months ago, you _____ a mechanic.

   g) He _____ an actor now, but two months ago, he _____ a shop assistant.

   h) Mary _____ a housewife, but two weeks ago, she _____ a librarian.

   i) They _____ students now, but last year, they _____ workers on a shipyard.

   j) Noreen _____ an executive assistant now, but two years ago, she _____ a student.

ENGLISH GRAMMAR PRACTICE

2. *Where were they on Monday? Make sentences:*

a) at school at 9 am.

b) in the cinema at four pm.

c) in hospital at noon.

d) on the bus at 8 am

e) at John's anniversary in the evening

f) with friends at the theatre at nine pm

g) at the baker's at two pm

h) at the newsagent's at 6 am

i) on the plane at four pm

j) in their car at ten am

3. *Complete the questions using **was** and **were**:*

a) Where _____ you on Thursday afternoon?

b) Where _____ she last Monday?

c) Where _____ they last month?

d) Where _____ he last year?

e) Where _____ you when I phoned you?

f) Where _____ she when you came?

g) Where _____ you when they looked for you?

h) Where _____ Mary and John when you called on them?

i) Where _____ I when you brought that book?

j) Where _____ we when the house was broken in?

ENGLISH GRAMMAR PRACTICE

4. Write the **-ed** forms of these verbs:

dance	cry	walk	talk
live	study	arrange	answer
die	dye	settle	ask

5. (a) Mrs. Lockwood does some things every day. Read what she does:

She wakes up at seven o'clock in the morning and goes to the bathroom. Then she prepares breakfast for the family and the sandwiches for school for her children. Then she drives her children to school. After leaving them at school, she goes shopping. When she comes back home, she cleans the house and prepares lunch for her children and herself. Then she does the washing up. In the afternoon, she reads a magazine or watch TV. Sometimes she does the laundry and irons clothes or helps her children with their homework. In the evening, she prepares dinner for the entire family because her husband comes back from work. She goes to bed at eleven o'clock.

(b) What did she do yesterday?

6. Complete the sentences with **did**, **have** or **had**:

a) What _____ you do yesterday? - I _____ an invitation to the cinema.

b) What _____ you have for breakfast yesterday? – I _____ tea.

c) What _____ you do in the test on Monday? I _____ well.

d) You _____ a meeting yesterday. _____ you forget?

e) She _____n't listen to the teacher in class yesterday.

f) They _____ their best as usual.

g) We _____ a boat two years ago. _____ you sail a lot? - Yes, we ____.

h) Martin and John _____ fight in the yard an hour ago.

i) I _____ a white sports car a few years ago.

j) The child _____ bread and butter for his snack yesterday.

7. *Complete the questions:*

a) where / they/go/last year?
b) what time/he/wake up/yesterday?
c) where / he / spend / his / vacation?
d) Lucy / come / to you / yesterday?
e) you /leave / early / for school/last year?
f) when / Joshua and Mary / meet / in the park / yesterday?
g) How long ago / you / study / French?
h) they / introduce / her / to you?
i) where / the boys / play / football/last Sunday?
j) they / sell/ the house /last month?

8. Match the answers with the questions:

a) When did you meet them?
b) What did you do in summer?
c) Why didn't you do your homework?
d) What time did they go there?
e) Did he come back from Paris last week?
f) Why did they lose their temper?
g) Did she succeed in her exams?
h) Who did they send the book to?
i) What time did the show start last night?
j) Did you buy the newspaper in the morning?

1) I didn't know the exercise.
2) No, he didn't. He came back two weeks ago.
3) Yes, she did.
4) I met them in winter last year.
5) It started at eight pm.
6) They sent it to their friends.
7) They went there in the morning the other day.
8) I went with friends to mountains.
9) No, I'm sorry. I forgot. I know it is too late now.
10) Because she did that stupid thing.

9. You are telling Tom about last Saturday evening. Complete sentences. Use the verbs: **invite**, **watch**, **sit**, **see**, **listen**, **cook**, **stand**, **tell**, **knock**, **bark**, **open**, **laugh**, **have**, **leave** and **wash**. Use the **simple past tense** or **past tense continuous**:

a) While we _____TV, someone _____ at the door.

b) Our dog _____ in the yard.

c) When I _____ the door, I _____ John, our neighbour, who _____ in front of the door.

d) I _____ to what he _____ me and I _____ him to sit down.

e) He _____ down and _____ me about what _____ to him.

f) After he _____, I _____ the dinner. '

g) They _____ TV, while I _____ dinner.

h) Then, I _____ the dishes.

i) While I _____ the dishes, the others _____ TV and they _____.

j) I _____ the kitchen too, and _____ TV with them afterwards.

ENGLISH GRAMMAR PRACTICE

10. Choose the word or phrase from each pair underlined in each sentence:

a) He <u>read</u> / <u>was reading</u> while Mary <u>cleaned</u> / <u>was cleaning</u> the bathroom.

b) She <u>wrote</u> / <u>was writing</u> a letter when she <u>was</u> / <u>was being</u> on vacation.

c) I <u>saw</u> / <u>was seeing</u> Alice just as she <u>get</u> / <u>was getting</u> into the office.

d) The dog <u>barked</u> / <u>was barking</u> when the thief <u>broke</u> / <u>was breaking</u> into the house.

e) He <u>told</u> / <u>was telling</u> that story when we <u>went</u> / <u>were going</u> together on the trip.

f) I <u>listened</u> / <u>was listening</u> to the tape when mother <u>arrived</u> / <u>was arriving</u>.

g) While Mary <u>cleaned</u> / <u>was cleaning</u> the house, Elaine <u>dusted</u> / <u>was dusting</u> the furniture.

h) Adrian <u>saw</u> / <u>was seeing</u> them when they <u>walked</u> / <u>were walking</u> in the park.

i) Father <u>dug</u> / <u>was digging</u> in the garden when it <u>started</u> / <u>was starting</u> to rain.

a) Mrs. Smith <u>read</u> / <u>was reading</u> a report when her secretary <u>entered</u> / <u>was entering</u> the room.

11. *Choose the correct word or phrase from each pair underlined in each sentence:*

- a) The boy played / was playing football when his father came / was coming home.
- b) She listened / was listening to the radio when I got / was getting into the room.
- c) While I drew / was drawing, the pencil-case fell / was falling.
- d) She drove / was driving to the sea when a police officer stopped / was stopping her.
- e) Wendy played / was playing the piano while Maria played / was playing the violin.
- f) When he entered / was entering the office, the secretary typed / was typing a letter.
- g) While they swam / were swimming, it started / was starting to rain.
- h) The children talked / were talking when the teacher came / was coming.
- i) He taught / was teaching the new lesson when Mary knocked / was knocking on the door.
- j) Louise talked / was talking over the telephone when her mother came / was coming back home.

12. *Choose the most appropriate word from each pair underlined in each sentence:*

a) She was driving when / while she saw the accident.
b) He saw the girl just as / when she was getting into the room.
c) She was writing a letter while / the moment the bell rang.
d) I saw a few fellows in front of the theatre just as / when I went to meet her.
e) The woman was reading a good novel as soon as / when the telephone rang.
f) She saw her two weeks on Sunday / ago.
g) Yesterday, I saw Alice when / while I was walking in the street.
h) They saw him the other day / recently.
i) Sheila was leaving the house once / when I came back.
j) I didn't read that book yesterday / lately.

UNIT 7: PRACTICE PAST TENSES - 2

1. Choose the correct word or phrase from each pair underlined:

a) John lived / was living at the country last year.
b) Sue and Ann came to us while we had / were having lunch.
c) He drove / was driving to the country when he had / was having the accident.
d) The riders stopped / were stopping on the top of the hill when they heard / were hearing that scream.
e) The woman left / was leaving the shop when she saw / was seeing the coat.
f) They built / were building a vacation house last year.
g) We ate / were eating when Aunt Mary dropped by/ was dropping by.
h) Lucy and Dan played / were playing cards while their brother watched / was watching TV.
i) When I left / was leaving the house, it rained / was raining hard and the wind blew / was blowing.
j) The class started / had started when he came / had come.

ENGLISH GRAMMAR PRACTICE

2. Rewrite each sentence according to the instructions given.

a) They left the house and drove to work at ten o'clock yesterday. (question)
b) Susan and David came to us the other day. (negative)
c) They didn't agree with his idea at the meeting on Thursday. (affirmative)
d) She didn't buy a new dress last week. (affirmative)
e) We drove to work yesterday morning. (negative)
f) Joshua spent a lot of money the other day. (negative)
g) They booked tickets for Paris last week. (question)
h) She never left the town last year. (question)
i) We went to the sea last summer. (negative)
j) She was telling the truth during the investigation. (question)

3. Complete each sentence with a suitable time expression from the list.
(you can use an expression more than once):

at, just as, when, last, while, ago, last year

a) He went there _____ I was waiting for him.
b) She saw the boy _____ he was getting into the car.
c) We met in London years _____.
d) _____ they opened a bookshop in our town.
e) They met in front of the station _____ 9:15.
f) How long _____ did you meet him at the hank?
g) She didn't pass her exams _____ month.

h) They were riding their bikes _____ the time.
i) I left the room _____ he entered.
j) Susie came to us an hour _____ .

4. Choose which sentence from 1) to 10) is the best continuation for the conversations beginning from a) to j):

a) Did Alice come to you the other day?
b) When did you meet John in town?
c) Did they leave the country?
d) When did you book the tickets for your vacation?
e) Did they like the play? What do you think?
f) Did you solve that issue?
g) Where did you go when you left the classes yesterday?
h) Why didn't you come to us on Friday?
i) Did he write you a letter? I think he promised.
j) Laura returned from abroad. She finished the university.

1) Yes, they did, indeed. Last week.
2) No, I didn't. Hannah tried to help me, but I didn't solve it.
3) I wasn't in town that's all.
4) I met my aunt in town. She came from the country.
5) Oh, yes, she did. She stayed for half an hour.
6) Yes, he did, but I haven't received anything yet.
7) I think so. They laughed a lot during the show.
8) Did she? That is good for her. What did she do there?
9) Last week I think.
10) Two weeks ago, maybe. I wanted badly to go there.

ENGLISH GRAMMAR PRACTICE

5. Put each verb given into either past simple or past continuous:

a) Lucy _____ (come) to us yesterday afternoon while we _____ (watch) the match on TV.

b) She _____ (iron) all the clothes while Fred _____ (dig) the garden.

c) We _____ (not come) to your party on Saturday because we _____ (have) a problem with the child.

d) Why _____ (I, not write) to you? Well, I don't know. Maybe I _____ (not have) time.

e) Louise _____ (feel) bad yesterday and she _____ (lie) in bed all day. She _____ (still, lie) in bed when I _____ (come).

f) They _____ (learn) French last year with Mrs. Denis. They _____ (like) her a lot. She _____ (teach) well.

g) The children _____ (play) in the garden when their mother _____ (call) them in.

h) While I _____ (write) my essay, the dog _____ (start) to bark. He _____ (bark) to a man at the door.

i) They _____ (not write) to her a line at least and, therefore, she _____ (get) very angry with them.

ENGLISH GRAMMAR PRACTICE

j) He _____ (always, talk) about race cars and that _____ (annoy) Mary.

6. Choose the correct spelling from each pair of words:

lyed / laid
tought / taught
spended / spent

meaned / meant
received / receivt
askt / asked

eated / ate
travelled / traveled
selled / sold

7. Put each verb given into either past simple or past continuous:

a) We _____ (phone) to the police when we _____ (see) the accident.

b) Josephine _____ (write) a letter to her friend in the country when John _____ (come) and _____ (invite) her to a show.

c) Alan and I _____ (meet) in the street the other day. I _____ (go) to my friend Jill at that moment.

d) Lucy and Dan _____ (get out) of the car when we _____ (see) them and _____ (call) their names.

e) Mr. Jones _____ (dictate) a letter to his assistant, Miss Smith, when the inspector _____ (come) in.

f) When I _____ (be) younger, I _____ (go) to the Black Sea and _____ (meet) John on the beach.

g) Rita _____ (play) chess with Richard when they _____ (hear) the dog barking.

h) The two young people _____ (talk) when the waitress _____ (lay) the plates on the table.

i) He _____ (try) to solve a problem when Mary (call) him up and _____ (ask) him about the result of the problem.

j) They _____ (have) a picnic when suddenly it _____ (start) to rain.

8. Choose the correct word or phrase underlined:

a) What did you do / were you doing when he knocked / was knocking at your door yesterday?

b) When did he live / was he living with you?

c) While he ate / was eating, what happened / was happening?

d) She bought / was buying a pair of socks in the shop when she heard / was hearing the fire alarm and she ran / was running out of the shop.

e) They answered / were answering to the questions of the quiz when the bell rang / was ringing and they stopped / were stopping.

f) Louise and I lived / were living with some friends that summer.

g) We realised / were realising that we had forgotten the bags in the car when we got / were getting inside.
h) It snowed / was snowing when the boys went / were going skiing.
i) The cat stole / was stealing the meat on the table when mother turned / was turning her back.
j) Their baby cried / was crying when we dropped / were dropping in.

9. Underline the error or the errors in each sentence and rewrite the sentences correctly:

a) They lay in bed when the bell was ringing. They worked a lot all that evening.
b) John heard he came in town two days ago and went to see him.
c) She never believed the story until she saw them and then she realised they said the truth.
d) We remembered they came to us before but we couldn't remember their faces.
e) She was driven down the road when she saw the kitten in the shadow of a tree.
f) They already left when we came to their house.
g) The boy slept all day yesterday and he didn't wake up when his parents came in the evening.
h) The teacher brought the tests they passed the day before.
i) He was going to the beach when he were young.
j) When he was a child, he was going to his grandparents every summer.

ENGLISH GRAMMAR PRACTICE

10. Choose the correct word or phrase underlined in each sentence:

a) I thought / was thinking I had the keys in my pocket but when I got / was getting to school I realised I forgot / had forgotten them at home.

b) They were sure they did / had done well in the test but when the teacher was bringing / brought the tests they realised they made / had made a lot of mistakes.

c) She met / was meeting them in the street yesterday and told / was telling them what she did / had done the day before.

d) We rode / were riding our horses across the fields and we laughed / were laughing when suddenly we saw the clouds in the sky.

e) Mary left / was leaving the house when we came / were coming to visit her. She said she already got / had already got an invitation to Mrs. Smith for tea and she had to leave.

f) The child took / had taken his bag and left / had left as soon as he ate / had eaten.

g) He was digging / had been digging in the garden all day long and he was very tired when we came / were coming.

h) John and Ann remembered they met / had met him somewhere before.

i) Alice and Dan were sure they won / had won in the lottery and they had.

ENGLISH GRAMMAR PRACTICE

j) When he <u>came</u> / <u>was coming,</u> he asked me what I <u>was doing</u> / <u>had been doing</u> all afternoon. I answered that I <u>was writing</u> / <u>had been writing</u> letters.

11. Put each verb into past simple, past continuous, past perfect or past perfect continuous:

a) We _____ (go) to see the film last evening when our car _____ (break) in the middle of the road.

b) She _____ (realise) she _____ (forget) to post the letter and she had to go back to the post-office.

c) The old man _____ (cross) the street to go to the chemist's when the car _____ (come) down the road and _____ (hit) him.

d) She _____ (lie) in bed all afternoon when I _____ (phone) her to see what she _____ (do).

e) The two boys _____ (play) football for two hours when the rain _____ (come) down fast.

f) I _____ (never, see) her before but I _____ (think) that her face _____ (look) familiar to me.

g) My sister and I _____ (play) cards since noon, when mother _____ (come) and _____ (tell) us to do our homework.

h) We _____ (go) to Mary's house as soon as we _____ (finish) our homework.

i) By the time she _____ (get) there, everyone _____ (leave).

j) They _____ (eat) anything until their mother _____ (come) home from work that day.

12. Complete each sentence using **would** or **used to** or **wouldn't** or **didn't use to**. More than one answer may be possible. Explain why.

   a) She _____ go to the sea every summer when she was very young.
   b) He _____ eat anything when he was nervous.
   c) I _____ hate schooldays when I was in the fifth form.
   d) They _____ come to school late every day when they were in school.
   e) We _____ visit her too often because we _____ like her at all.
   f) She _____ always do such a thing in those days.
   g) Alex and Tom _____ love the same girl last year.
   h) I _____ go skiing every winter in my youth.
   i) You _____ like this kind of food very much, indeed, when you were a child.
   j) He _____ spend one month a year in his friends' house in the mountains.

ENGLISH GRAMMAR PRACTICE

13. Rephrase the sentence using the word given in brackets, but keeping the same meaning:

a) She couldn't get into the house because her keys were in the bag on the
kitchen table at home. (**FORGET**)

b) She was a real bother for us because she forgot everything (**ALWAYS**)

c) They got into the house and Mary came at once. (**NO SOONER**)

d) That was the best meal she had ever cooked and I had ever eaten. (**NEVER**)

e) She entered the house and then the telephone rang. (**JUST**)

f) The dog got up and then the boy put a bone onto his plate. (**SCARCELY**)

g) He told me the most stupid thing ever and I couldn't believe my ears. (**NEVER**)

h) The baby fell and I tried to catch it at once. (**ALREADY**)

i) We got there to see him but he wasn't there anymore. (**BY**)

j) I entered the house first and I had to leave again.
(HARDLY)

14. *Choose the correct word or phrase underlined:*

   a) No sooner <u>had I got</u> / <u>I had got</u> into the house than the phone <u>rang</u> / <u>was ringing</u>.
   b) They <u>reached</u> / <u>had reached</u> the airport in the end but the plane <u>already left</u> / <u>had already left</u>.
   c) That was the first coffee the woman <u>drank</u> / <u>had drunk</u> that day.
   d) It was the most embarrassing situation I <u>ever saw</u> / <u>had ever seen</u>.
   e) She <u>drove</u> / <u>was driving</u> / <u>had been driving</u> to the town when she realised she <u>forgot</u> / <u>had forgotten</u> to fill the tank.
   f) We <u>read</u> / <u>were reading</u> / <u>had been reading</u> all evening when he <u>got</u> / <u>was getting</u> / <u>had got</u> into the house.
   g) When the sun <u>rose</u> / <u>was rising</u>, he <u>walked</u> / <u>was walking</u> / <u>had been walking</u> on the beach for half an hour already.
   h) By the time he <u>got</u> / <u>had got</u> back home, the police <u>left</u> / <u>had left</u>.
   i) Helen <u>slept</u> / <u>had slept</u> / <u>had been sleeping</u> by the time we <u>got</u> / <u>had got</u> there.
   j) They <u>sent</u> / <u>had sent</u> us a reply to our letter as soon as they <u>received</u> / <u>had received</u> it.

UNIT 8: CONSOLIDATION PAST TENSE

1. Choose the most suitable words underlined:

a) Mark came / was coming to her the moment she left / was leaving the office to go home.

b) She was going / would go to the Porters every summer when she was / was being in the 5th form.

c) Linda and Diane left / were leaving the cinema hall when we saw / were seeing them.

d) Nathan and I had come / came here by the time he moved / had moved into the school.

e) I didn't notice / wasn't noticing anything but he told / was telling me what happened / had happened before my arrival.

f) Everyone cried / was crying and shouted / was shouting and no one kept / was keeping cool in the room.

g) We never saw / had never seen such an interesting play before and therefore we recommended / had recommended it to our friends.

h) The girls talked / were talking while the teacher explained / was explaining the lesson and, therefore, he got / was getting very upset.

i) He used to like / would like swimming in the lake in his childhood.

j) Lucian didn't use to own / wouldn't own a car that year.

ENGLISH GRAMMAR PRACTICE

2. Put each verb in brackets into a suitable tense. All sentences refer to past time:

a) She _____ (never, visit) them before so they _____ (not meet) her until then.

b) We _____ (drive) to the country that morning and we _____ (meet) the Browns in an inn near Plymouth.

c) She _____ (book) tickets for Edinburgh that day. I _____ (see) her in the travel agent's when she _____ (pay) the tickets. She _____ (greet) me and we _____ (talk) for a while.

d) The accounting office _____ (complete) the work until the economic inspectors _____ (come).

e) She _____ (not used to) go with them those days because she _____ (not like) their company.

f) Sue Ellen _____ (come) home in the afternoon. She _____ (notice) at once her house (be broken) into.

g) The children _____ (play) cards all the afternoon when their mother _____ (come) home from work.

h) There were more people in the shop. Some people _____ (buy) some bread and cakes, others _____ (look around) for some food and the others _____ (expect) the new products to be exhibited.

ENGLISH GRAMMAR PRACTICE

i) George and Alan _____ (have) an appointment with their doctor that day and they _____ (meet) in order to go together.

j) Last week, they _____ (visit) the Smiths and _____ (have) fun together. They _____ (make) acquaintance long time ago and they _____ (spend) time together now and then.

3. Correct the sentences. Some of them may be correct:

a) We had never met him before and we had been amazed to see that he had been such a spoiled child.

b) The director would have a nice office with some new furniture and interesting decorations.

c) They didn't sleep when I had got into their room and I minded that.

d) You hadn't come with us in the park last Sunday. What was happening?

e) The dog was liking such a food and, therefore, I would give it to him at least every three days.

f) You had seen him before that night? – I hadn't, but I liked him at once.

g) When I was coming home, the cat was sleeping since morning.

h) The child was doing his homework since he was coming home.

i) She never saw such a beautiful flower before.

j) The climbers arrived at the cottage by noon.

ENGLISH GRAMMAR PRACTICE

4. Put each verb in brackets into a suitable past tense. Use the past perfect or past perfect continuous only where this is necessary:

a) They _____ (meet) that morning to go on a trip in the mountains. They _____ (be) there before and they _____ (really, like) the place.

b) They _____ (leave) early to catch the first bus. They _____ (take) rucksacks and torches with them.

c) They _____ (reach) the end of their trip by bus after they _____ (travel) for two hours.

d) They _____ (start) the climb and after two hours they _____ (reach) a nice cottage in a sunny valley.

e) They _____ (leave) the cottage after they _____ (eat) and _____ (drink) a little water.

f) They _____ (climb) for three hours when they _____ (get) onto the peak.

g) They _____ (rest) for a while before starting to walk again.

h) They _____ (walk) for more than four hours when they _____ (get) back to the bus station.

i) They _____ (take) the bus after they _____ (wait) for more than half an hour.

j) They _____ (arrive) in town by ten o'clock at night.

5. *In each sentence, decide whether one or both of the alternative tenses given are appropriate:*

a) No sooner had they received / they received the telegram than they booked / had booked the tickets for the plane.
b) They were working / had been working for five hours when the telephone rang / was ringing and interrupted / had interrupted them.
c) They didn't see / hadn't seen their aunt until they came / had come back in town.
d) She knitted / had knitted a pullover last year.
e) They bought / had bought new furniture for their bedroom after they moved / had moved into a new flat.
f) Their friends left / had already left the hotel when they arrived / had arrived at their hotel.
g) We graduated / had graduated high school by the time he became / had become a freshman.
h) Stan drove / was driving to the country when he had / was having an accident.
i) They didn't buy / hadn't bought the dresses they wanted / had wanted until they received / had received their pay cheque.
j) They already left / had already left when the teacher came / had come with the results of the test.

ENGLISH GRAMMAR PRACTICE

6. *Rewrite each sentence so that it contains the word or words in capitals given. Do not change the words in any way and keep the meaning:*

a) He left and then his sister came to ask for him. (**HAD**)
b) He fell in love: she was the most beautiful girl for him. (**EVER**)
c) They settled the tents and then they made the campfire at once. (**AS SOON AS**)
d) She woke up and started working at once. (**SCARCELY**)
e) Sheila and Joan went to their grandparents every holiday. (**WOULD**)
f) I had packed all the things when they came to pick me up. (**BY**)
g) The car crashed and the police came at once. (**AS SOON AS**)
h) The lecture ended and the students left the university in a minute. (**ONCE**)
i) As soon as he had finished decorating his cottage in the mountains, his cousin asked him to let him go there for a week. (**HARDLY**)
j) She drank a new glass of juice: it was the fourth. (**HAD**)

7. *Choose the most appropriate time expression underlined:*

a) He had left the schoolyard <u>when</u> / <u>just as</u> I came.
b) My brother and I would go to the camp <u>every holiday</u> / <u>scarcely</u>.
c) We realised that Joshua and Ann had met <u>before</u> / <u>at once</u>. They were good friends.
d) Lillian remembered she had forgotten the window open <u>when</u> / <u>as soon as</u> she left the house.
e) We had <u>already</u> / <u>no sooner</u> eaten by the time mother woke up.
f) The teacher had <u>just</u> / <u>soon</u> entered the classroom <u>when</u> / <u>while</u> the fire alarm went off.
g) You had been reading <u>for</u> / <u>since</u> noon when we came, hadn't you?
h) I had seen the play <u>before</u> / <u>at once</u> and therefore, I told them to go too.
i) He was tired because he had been reading the reports <u>before</u> / <u>all night</u>.
j) She recognized him <u>at once</u> / <u>no sooner</u>. He was the man who smiled to her in the train.

ENGLISH GRAMMAR PRACTICE

8. *Choose the most suitable words underlined:*

a) No sooner had he put/ he had put the receiver in the hook than the phone rang / was ringing again.

b) They put / were putting their books into their bags as soon as the class ended / had ended.

c) The child bought / had bought the books by the time I came / had come home.

d) No one believed / had believed when he told / was telling us what happened / had happened / was happening the day before.

e) The sun already set / had already set down when the group got / was getting into the glade.

f) We got / were getting into the cinema hall when he saw / had seen us. We entered / had entered together and sat / had sat down. When the lights went / had gone out the film started / had started.

g) The vase with flowers fell / was falling off the table on the floor when the cat hit / was hitting it.

h) The children had entered / entered the house as soon as the wind had started / started to blow and it had started / started to rain.

i) They used to / would like going to the beach on sunny days.

j) No one understood / had understood what he said / was saying because the noise was overwhelming.

UNIT 9: PRESENT PERFECT TENSE AND PRESENT PERFECT CONTINUOUS

EXPLANATIONS
PRESENT PERFECT TENSE

A) Situations

1. To express an action in the past when we do not know the moment of occurrence, we use present perfect tense.

> Ex1: They went to the sea **last year**. (simple past → the moment is mentioned)
>
> Ex2: They have gone to the sea. (moment not mentioned → present perfect tense)

Observation: *If we are interested in the place of the action and not in the moment of the action, we use simple past tense.*

> Ex: I have bought the book. *I bought it from* **Dallas**.

2. The action has just taken place or has already ended → present perfect tense

NOTE: JUST and **ALREADY** appear in the sentence.

> Ex1: He has *just* drunk his coffee.
>
> Ex2: He has *already* drunk his coffee.

3. The action started in the past and has not ended yet → present perfect

NOTE: *Generally, the verb is in the negative and* **YET** *is added at the end of the sentence (however, the verb might be in affirmative, sometimes)*

Ex: He hasn't learnt for the exam *yet*.

4. The action presents repeatability in the past and it might take place in the present too → present perfect

Ex: He's gone to see that film *twice*.

5. The adverb *NEVER* is present in the sentence and no other moment is mentioned → present perfect tense

Ex1: He has *never* read that novel.
Ex2: He *never* met her *last year*. (simple past because of *last year*)

6. The adverb *EVER* is present and no other moment is mentioned → present perfect tense

Ex1: Have you *ever* read his work?
Ex2: Did you *ever* see him *when you were young*? (simple past because the time of the action is mentioned by the sentence *when you were young*)

7. The adverb *BEFORE* is present in the sentence and no other mention of the time is present → present perfect

Ex1: I have not seen this play *before.*

Ex2: I didn't see the letter *before he came.* (simple past → *before he came expresses the moment*)

8. SO FAR, UP TO NOW, RECENTLY, LATELY → require present perfect tense

Ex: *Lately* I have learnt for exams.

9. A phrase like: IT'S THE FIRST TIME, IT'S THE SECOND TIME, IT'S THE THRID TIME, etc. requires present perfect tense in the clause.

Ex: *It's the first time* I have laid my eyes on him.

NOTE: *The expression* **IT'S THE LAST TIME** *shows that the action does not take place again* → ***simple past tense***

10. If in the sentence whose verb is in present tense there is a noun accompanied by an ordinal numeral, in its clause, we use present perfect tense

Ex: It's *the second coffee* I have drunk.

NOTE: *If the noun is accompanied by* **THE LAST**: *1) the action ended* → *simple past tense; 2) the action is happening now* → *simple present tense or present continuous*

11. If there is a noun in the sentence with the verb in present tense and it is accompanied by an adjective in superlative → present perfect tense in the clause + adverb *EVER*

Ex: He's *the most obstinate* man I have ever seen.

12. When the period in which the action takes place is not concluded → present perfect tense

Ex1: *It's ten o'clock.* I have looked for him twice this morning.

(*it's ten o'clock = still morning*)

Ex2: *It's one o'clock.* I looked for him twice this morning.

(*it's one o'clock → morning ended, period concluded*)

13. *SINCE* or *FOR* is present in the sentence → present perfect tense

Ex: I have called him *since* one o'clock.

NOTE: *If* **SINCE** *or* **FOR** *introduces a clause sentence →* **present perfect** *in the main sentence and* **simple past** *in the clause sentence*

Ex: I have met him *since* he came in this town.

NOTE: *There are situations when we have to use* **present perfect continuous** *when* **SINCE** *or* **FOR** *are present in the sentence*

Ex: I have been walking *for* hours!

14. We use present perfect to show the anteriority of the clause sentence when we have future in the main sentence.

Ex: I will come after I have finished.

Observation: we can use present simple in the time clause, though.

Ex: I will come after I finish.

15. We use simple present perfect to show an action in the past that has a consequence in the present.

Ex: They are punished. They've broken John's bike.

(*they are punished* – consequence in the present)

Pay attention to the difference between HAVE BEEN and HAVE GONE!!!

HAVE GONE

– **shows that the action has not ended and that the person has not come back yet**

Ex: I've gone to London. (*that means: I'm still there*)

HAVE BEEN

- **shows that the action ended**

Ex: I've been to London this week. (*that means: I 've actually come back*)

B) Conjugation of verbs

NOTE: *All perfect tenses use in conjugation the auxiliary TO HAVE (in present, past, future – depending on the time of the action) + the verb in the third form* ➔ *for present perfect, we use TO HAVE in present + the 3rd form of the verb*

1. Affirmative

Subject + have / has + the third form of the verb

Ex: I have worked since breakfast.

   I've worked since breakfast. (short form)

Ex: He has just come back.

   He's just come back. (short form)

2. Negative

Subject + have not / has not + third form verb

Subject + haven't / hasn't + third form verb

Ex: I haven't learnt for the exam yet.

Ex: He hasn't sent the parcel to them yet.

3. Interrogative

Have / Has + subject + third form verb?

Ex: Have they had dinner yet?

Ex: Has he returned the books yet?

4. Interrogative – Negative

Have / Has + subject + not + third form verb?

Haven't / Hasn't + subject + third form verb?

Ex: Haven't you gone there yet?

Ex: Hasn't he listened to that tape yet?

PRESENT PERFECT CONTINUOUS

A. Situations

1. A verb in the present perfect continuous expresses mainly and action coming from the past and connected to the present.

Ex: I'm sorry for the mess, but I've been cleaning the house *for the last twenty minutes*.

2. We may use the present perfect continuous to emphasize the duration of the action.

Ex: I've been staying here a lot! Where have you been?

3. We may use present perfect continuous to emphasize the fact that the action is very recent.

Ex: I've been washing clothes! *I've just finished*.

4. We may use present perfect continuous to emphasize a temporary action.

Ex: I've been working with them *for the past week*.

5. We may express a recent action using the present perfect continuous.

Ex: I've been reading a lot, that's all.

6. Present perfect continuous shows that an action from the past continues in the present.

Ex: *I'm reading*. I've been reading *all morning*.

7. We use the present perfect continuous to show a repeated action or to show that an action takes place too often.

Ex: He's been bothering me *three times* this week!

Time expressions used in present perfect continuous in such a situation:

    a) All day, all morning etc.

    b) For ages, for weeks, etc.

    c) Lately, recently

Compare with present perfect:

    Ex1: I've read *ten* articles. (action already ended: number of articles is mentioned).

    Ex2: I've been reading articles. (the action keeps going on)

A) Conjugation

NOTE:

It is a perfect tense ➔ auxiliary TO HAVE + third form of the verb

It is a continuous aspect of a tense ➔ auxiliary TO BE + [vb+-ING]

➔ we conjugate TO BE in the present perfect and we add [vb+-ING]

1. Affirmative

    Subject + have/has + been + [verb + -ING]

Ex: I have been reading all morning.

       I've been reading all morning.

Ex: He has been playing football all afternoon.

He's been playing football all afternoon.

2. Negative

Subject + have / has + not + been + [verb +-ING]

Subject + haven't / hasn't + been + [verb + -ING]

Ex: I haven't been listening to music all the time.

Ex: He hasn't been driving all morning.

3. Interrogative

Have/Has + subject + been + [verb + -ING]?

Ex: Have you been waiting here all this time?

Ex: Has he been playing on line games all this afternoon?

4. Interrogative – Negative

Have / Has + subject + not + been + [verb + -ING]?

Haven't / Hasn't + subject + been + [verb + -ING]?

Ex: Haven't you been doing anything all this day?

Ex: Hasn't he been listening to anything the professor is saying?

UNIT 10: PRACTICE PRESENT PERFECT - 1

1. Complete what Mary says. Use the present perfect simple or continuous and **for** and **since**:

a) I'm from England but I live in Paris now. I _____ (live) here _____ 1996.

b) I'm a broker. I work for an insurance company in Paris. I _____ (work) there _____ five years.

c) I'm married to Tom. We _____ (be) married _____ 1992.

d) Tom is a teacher. He _____ _____ five years already.

e) We _____ (live) in the same house _____ two years.

f) We _____ (buy) our car _____ 1992.

g) We are going on vacation in Greece this year. We _____ (plan) this vacation _____ two months.

h) We _____ (book) the tickets _____ two weeks now.

i) Tom _____ (invite) his sister to go with us _____ last month.

ENGLISH GRAMMAR PRACTICE

j) She _____ (make) plans for the trip ever since.

2. Mary's answers are in the exercise number 1. You ask the appropriate questions to obtain the respective answers.

3. Make sentences or questions using the words given below:

a) You / eat / exotic food / ever?
b) He / leave / since noon / with Tom
c) I / never / be / here / before
d) She / just / do / her homework / and / already / go out
e) I / walk / with Mary / in the park / for / one hour
f) How long / she / write / on this novel?
g) We / work / in the same place / for / five years
h) She / wait / for me / for / half an hour
i) They / read / in their room / for three hours
j) She / never / meet / Dan / before

4. Answer the questions below using the words in brackets:

a) Are you washing your clothes now? (*already*)
b) Is Dan listening to the news now? (*just*)
c) Is she ironing the tablecloth now? (*before*)
d) Is the teacher in his office now? (*just*)
e) Are they playing cards in their room now? (*so far*)
f) Is she going to buy the newspaper? (*already*)
g) Is mother writing letters this afternoon? (*before*)

h) Are the children sleeping now? (*up to now*)
i) Are they having breakfast at the moment? (*just*)
j) Is Alan seeing his friends off to the bus stop? (*before*)

5. Choose the correct word or phrase underlined in each sentence:

a) They didn't learn / haven't learnt for the exam yet.
b) The child read / has read the novel an hour ago.
c) She wrote / has written the letters so far.
d) They did / have done their homework for an hour.
e) I visited / have visited them before lunch.
f) We heard / have heard the news before.
g) They left / have left since noon and they didn't come back / haven't come back yet.
h) They went / have gone to walk in the woods yesterday.
i) Lucy drove / has driven to the country the other day.
j) She cooked / has cooked dinner up to now.

ENGLISH GRAMMAR PRACTICE

6. Put each verb given in either present perfect simple, present perfect continuous, past simple or present simple:

a) It is the first time she _____ (come) here in her life.

b) This evening, the boy _____ (not eat) anything yet but he usually _____ (eat) quite a lot in the evening.

c) I _____ (come) to this school since we _____ (move) into this neighbourhood.

d) They _____ (learn) well at school and _____ (do) all their homework. Today they _____ (work) since four o'clock.

e) I _____ (not have) a car last year. I _____ (buy) my car in April.

f) I _____ (usually, not drink) tea in the morning, but yesterday I _____ (drink) some.

g) Last year, we _____ (drive) to the sea and the trip _____ (take) five hours. Today, we _____ (drive) to the sea for two hours and we _____ (already, pass) by your town.

h) They _____ (call) us up at three or four everyday, but today they _____ (not call) so far and it's about six in the evening.

i) They are the most intelligent students I _____ (ever, have).

j) I _____ (have) an old car last year and it _____ (not run) very well. I _____ (buy) a new one in March and it _____ (run) just fine ever since.

7. Complete each mini-dialogue using the verbs given in either present perfect simple, present perfect continuous, present simple or simple past:

a) *Crossing Jordan* is tonight on TV. _____ (you, ever, see) it? – No, not yet. Is it good?

b) When _____ (you, go) there last time? – I _____ (not know) for sure, but I think I _____ (not be) there for two years.

c) _____ (You, see) him recently? – No, I _____ (not see) him for a few days, I suppose.

d) May I see Ellen? Is she at home? – No, I'm afraid _____ (you, miss) her. She _____ (leave) a few moments ago.

e) Where _____ (you, be) at noon yesterday? – At school, I think. Why? – I _____ (want) to talk to you and I _____ (not find) you anywhere.

f) How long _____ (you study) French? – For five years. Why? – You _____ (speak) very well.

g) _____ (you, see) Mary lately? – No, I haven't. Why? – I _____ (hear) she is in hospital. She _____ (break) her leg.

h) Where _____ (your brother, be) the other day? – I _____ (not know) for sure, but I _____ (suppose) he _____ (play) football with his pals.

i) _____ (you, read) anything interesting lately? – Actually, I have. I _____ (read) Ludlum's new book.

j) _____ (you, read) my offer? – Yes, but I _____ (not think) it _____ (fit) our interests.

8. Put **one** suitable word in each space:

a) John has left _____ so you can't see him.

b) I haven't met him _____ so I don't know too much about him.

c) Alice and Dan made acquaintance _____ March last year and they have been friends _____ _____.

d) Carla and I left _____ yesterday morning, but we got late to school.

e) _____ _____ I haven't done too much in the house. I have had no time.

f) She has _____ gone to bed but I'll wake her up if you want.

g) Denis and I met _____ night in town and went together to a restaurant.

h) We have missed the plane, I'm afraid. It has _____ taken off.

i) I have _____ heard some interesting news. Mary has won two competitions _____.

j) We haven't seen this movie _____ so we'll enjoy it.

UNIT 11: PRACTICE PRESENT PERFECT – 2

1. *Choose the correct word or phrase underlined:*

a) I wrote / have written / have been writing translation exercises all morning.

b) He is reading / has been reading all evening. I think he goes / has gone / is going to bed soon.

c) The girl talks / is talking / has been talking on the phone. I think she talks / is talking / has been talking for twenty minutes now.

d) Joshua is sleeping / slept / has been sleeping all afternoon.

e) He went / has gone / is going to bed a few moments ago.

f) They come / have come / are coming to us this evening. – They came / have come / have been coming to you all week.

g) Are you seeing / Do you see John there? – Yes, I think he waits / has been waiting / is waiting for someone. He stays / is staying / has been staying there for twenty minutes. I watched / have watched / have been watching him all this time.

h) What do you do / are you doing? – I listen / am listening / have been listening to a concert on the radio. I listened / have listened / have been listening to it for an hour.

ENGLISH GRAMMAR PRACTICE

i) The boy <u>writes</u> / <u>has written</u> / <u>has been writing</u> letters since two o'clock.

j) What <u>does Mary do</u> / <u>is Mary doing</u> / <u>has Mary been doing</u>? – She <u>writes</u> / <u>is writing</u> / <u>has been writing</u> her reports. She <u>is writing</u> / <u>has been writing</u> / <u>wrote</u> for two hours.

2. *Put the verbs given is simple present, present continuous, present perfect, present perfect continuous or simple past:*

a) Mel _____ (leave) by car for Berlin at noon. He _____ (drive) since noon. He _____ (arrive) yet.

b) What _____ (you, listen) to? – I'm listening to an English language tape. I _____ (listen) to it since breakfast. I _____ (listen) to six lessons already.

c) David _____ (play) football. He _____ (play) for two hours. He _____ (play) yesterday too.

d) She _____ (just, come) inside. She _____ (walk) for a while. She _____ (usually, walk) in the afternoon.

e) The girls _____ (have) a chat. They _____ (talk) for two hours. They _____ (meet) in the afternoons and _____ (talk) for hours.

f) They _____ (go) to the cinema an hour ago. They _____ (be) in the cinema hall now. The film _____ (start). It _____ (run) for half an hour.

g) I _____ (go) to Maria's at three o'clock. We _____ (talk) for an hour and _____ (wait) for Anna to come too. She _____ (not come) yet.

h) The boys _____ (meet) once a week to play cards. They _____ (start) playing at five this afternoon. They _____ (play) now. They _____ (play) for two hours.

i) Alan _____ (sleep) now. He _____ (go) to bed half an hour ago. He _____ (sleep) for half an hour.

j) Mother _____ (wash) dishes. We _____ (just, have) dinner. We _____ (watch) TV. We _____ (watch) TV for a quarter of an hour.

ENGLISH GRAMMAR PRACTICE

3. Complete the second sentence so that it has a similar meaning to the first sentence.

a) They moved into our neighbourhood two years ago.

They _____ for _____.

b) I went for a walk at one o'clock.

I _____ since one o'clock.

c) He started learning English five years ago.

He _____ for five years.

d) Mary started to write this novel two years ago.

Mary _____ for two years.

e) We started working here in 1992.

We _____ since 1992.

f) She started reading at two o'clock.

She _____ since two o'clock.

g) It started raining in this area two weeks ago.

It _____ for two weeks.

h) He went to bed at three o'clock.

He _____ since three o'clock.

i) They started waiting for their guests at eleven o'clock and now it is noon.

They _____ for an hour.

j) She started washing the clothes at four o'clock and now it is six.

She _____ for two hours.

ENGLISH GRAMMAR PRACTICE

4. Correct the sentences below:

a) How long ago have you moved there?
b) Josh didn't come yet, I'm afraid.
c) I have been writing her address right now so have a seat for a minute.
d) When have he come to you last night?
e) I usually have written to him quite often.
f) She was doing her homework all afternoon and she hasn't finished yet.
g) Dan is coming to you last night.
h) I have ate a cake so far so I'll have another one.
i) We losted our books yesterday so we can't do our homework.
j) Lydia just left so you can't talk to her.

5. Choose the most appropriate time underlined:

a) He <u>goes</u> / <u>is going</u> / <u>has gone</u> out of the room angrily because he <u>has</u> / <u>has had</u> / <u>has been having</u> a fight with his brother.
b) John <u>broke</u> / <u>has broken</u> / <u>is breaking</u> his sister's toy the other day.
c) They <u>leave</u> / <u>left</u> / <u>have left</u> on a trip by car yesterday morning and they <u>visit</u> / <u>visited</u> / <u>have visited</u> two cities so far.
d) Our children <u>play</u> / <u>played</u> / <u>have played</u> with our neighbour's kids every day. They <u>play</u> / <u>have played</u> / <u>played</u> yesterday too. They <u>just come</u> / <u>are just</u>

coming / have just come / just came to play with them. They are out in the yard now.

e) She started / has started playing the violin an hour ago. She already played / has already played too much, don't you think?

f) Where is Mary? – She went / has gone out with her friends an hour ago. She is walking / has been walking for an hour.

g) I'm sorry I'm late. My watch stops / has stopped. I forget / forgot / have forgotten to wind it up last night.

h) I finished / have finished writing my reports for school, mother. May I go out? I go / am going with George to a film.

i) They drive / are driving / have been driving since ten o'clock in the morning. They already passed / have already passed by Brampton.

j) I can't do my homework, mother. I understood / have understood nothing in class today.

6. Choose the most appropriate tense from the forms underlined:

a) John slammed / **has slammed** the door behind him. He just had / **has just had** a row with Ann and he is furious.

b) We **went** / have gone to the sea last summer and this summer we went / **have gone** to the mountains.

c) The student just put / **has just** put his work on the teacher's desk and he **left** / has left the classroom.

d) I just finished / **have just finished** my letter to Mary. I **wrote** / have written ten pages.

e) I hear the dog barking. I think someone got / **has got** into our garden.

f) When I **came** / have come / had come home, I **saw** / have seen that there was a message on the answering machine. Someone called / **had called** / has called and left / **had left** / has left a message.

g) Finally, I have a little peace. Our neighbour's guests left / **have left** / had left and the music stopped / **has stopped** / had stopped.

h) When I got / have got / **had got** to the bus stop, people had waited / have waited / waited / **had been waiting** for half an hour and the bus didn't come / **hadn't come** / hasn't come yet.

i) Turn the tape, please, it ended / **has ended**.

j) Yesterday, it snowed / was snowing / **had been snowing** since morning and it didn't stop / **hadn't stopped** all day.

ENGLISH GRAMMAR PRACTICE

7. Complete the second sentence so that it has a similar meaning to the first sentence:

a) They have come to us since we met them there and they are still coming.

    They _____ we met them.

b) We've tried to fix the car since one o'clock and we are still working.

    We _____ since one o'clock.

c) He started giving his speech at two o'clock and he's still speaking.

    He _____ since two o'clock.

d) They've studied German since they came to this school and they are still studying it.

    They _____ since they came to this school.

e) She started playing the piano at three o'clock and she's still playing it.

    She _____ since three o'clock.

f) They moved in this town ten years ago and they are still leaving here.

    They _____ for ten years.

g) Mother started cooking lunch at ten o'clock and now it is twelve and she's still cooking it.

    Mother _____ for two hours.

h) He left by car for Cambridge at dawn and hasn't arrived yet.

    He _____ since dawn.

i) Oh, bother! He started reading the newspaper at breakfast and hasn't finished yet!

    Oh, bother! He _____ since breakfast.

ENGLISH GRAMMAR PRACTICE

j) The students started the test an hour ago and they are still writing.

The students _____ for an hour.

8. Complete each sentence a) to j) with an appropriate answer from 1) to 10). Do not use an answer more than once:

a) Do you know what they did the other day?	1) Yes, I did. She had been playing tapes when I came to her.
b) Have you solved the problem?	2) Yes, they have. I saw them a few minutes ago.
c) What was he doing when you came to his place on Monday?	3) Not yet, but I'm still looking for one.
d) Did you see her on Sunday?	4) Yes, I received two letters so far.
e) How long have you been studying German?	5) I'm not very sure, but I think they went to the swimming pool.
f) Did you notice anything strange when you got there?	6) Oh, yes! She left him.
g) Have they written to you?	7) Not yet, but I'm still trying.
h) They have left, haven't they?	8) For ten years and I think I manage quite well.
i) She did it, didn't she?	9) Yes, I think they were fighting.
j) Have you bought a car?	10) I think he was having a shower.

9. Complete the second sentence so that it has a similar meaning to the first sentence:

a) She went to the shops a moment ago.
   She _____ to the shops.
b) He came to learn in our university two months ago.
   He _____ for two months.
c) John has German classes since September.
   John _____ since September.
d) She is still doing her homework so she can't go out.
   She _____ yet, _____ out.
e) Mother left the house a moment ago and went to Aunt Alice.
   Mother _____ the house and _____ to Aunt Alice.
f) Five cakes are ready, mother.
   Mother, I _____ so far.
g) It's a long time since I met him for the last time.
   I _____ for a long time.
h) This is the first time John has gone to the sea.
   John _____ before.
i) I'm afraid I don't know what I have done with my wallet.
   I've _____, I'm afraid.
j) He doesn't agree with you anymore.
   He _____ mind _____.

10. Rewrite each sentence, beginning as shown, but keep the meaning of the first sentence:

a) I haven't seen him for ages.

   It's ages _____.

b) It's a long time since he was there for the last time.

   He hasn't _____.

c) This is his second concert in his lifetime.

   He has _____.

d) She is on the twentieth page on the book she's reading.

   She has _____.

e) They don't have their books in their bags.

   They have _____.

f) He was eating when I came and he started at nine.

   He had _____.

g) I moved here in 1989.

   I have _____.

h) We left to Paris by train at ten.

   We have _____.

i) She started knitting this pullover in March.

   She has _____.

j) She bought her bag in June and she was still wearing it in January.

   She had _____.

ENGLISH GRAMMAR PRACTICE

UNIT 12: PROGRESS TEST

1. Rewrite each sentence so that it contains the word in capitals, and so that the meaning stays the same:

a) I started playing the violin when I was five. (**HAVE**)

b) She started listening to that radio concert when she came back from school. (**BEEN**)

c) We are writing letters and we started an hour ago. (**HAVE**)

d) When I came, she finished writing her homework. (**BY**)

e) We came back home and then the telephone rang. (**SCARCELY**)

f) She used to be kind to her friends, but now she is quite rude. (**BEHAVIOUR**)

g) They stopped writing to us in March. (**HAD**)

h) We don't listen to music so often. (**STOPPED**)

i) Whose car is that? (**BELONG**)

j) Mary was drawing when I got there and I understood she started in the morning. (**BEEN**)

ENGLISH GRAMMAR PRACTICE

2. Choose the most appropriate phrase underlined for each situation:

a) Alice <u>has left</u> / <u>has been leaving</u> the office and she <u>has just got</u> / <u>has just been getting</u> into the car, he pointed out.

b) Daniel and Alex <u>have trained</u> / <u>have been training</u> in the gym all day long. They <u>haven't finished</u> / <u>didn't finish</u> yet.

c) Dorian and I <u>have waited</u> / <u>have been waiting</u> for Mary since one o'clock. I think we should leave.

d) The child <u>has slept</u> / <u>has been sleeping</u> all afternoon and <u>hasn't woken</u> / <u>hasn't been waking</u> up yet.

e) Marilee and Josh <u>have been married</u> / <u>are married</u> for thirty years.

f) Lucille <u>had worked</u> / <u>had been working</u> on that project for four hours when <u>we came</u> / <u>have come</u>.

g) I <u>had presented</u> / <u>had been presenting</u> the commercial twenty minutes when the fire alarm <u>had got off</u> / <u>got off</u>.

h) So far, we <u>didn't visit</u> / <u>haven't visited</u> the Art Museum, but this month we <u>visited</u> / <u>have visited</u> the History Museum twice.

i) Dan <u>lost</u> / <u>has lost</u> his wallet and he <u>was</u> / <u>is</u> broke. Can you lend him some money?

j) He <u>came</u> / <u>has come</u> last night and <u>asked</u> / <u>has asked</u> me the history book for a few days.

ENGLISH GRAMMAR PRACTICE

3. Choose the most suitable word or phrase underlined from each sentence:

a) Where have you been? I've waited / <u>I've been waiting</u> here for two hours.

b) <u>Have you learnt</u> / Have you been learning your lessons for tomorrow? – Yes, I have.

c) He <u>has been speaking</u> / has spoken to Mary on the phone since eight and he hasn't finished yet.

d) He has worked / <u>has been working</u> in his room since eight and he will continue to do so until four.

e) How long have you been living / <u>have you lived</u> in this town? <u>I've lived</u> / I've been living here since 1987 and I will continue to do so.

f) The TV is on. He is in front of the TV. He's watched / <u>He's been watching</u> TV for a long time.

g) George is putting his pen down on the desk. <u>He's just finished</u> / He's just been finishing his homework.

h) The teacher is speaking to his students. He's spoken / <u>He's been speaking</u> for half an hour.

i) <u>They've been swimming</u> / They've swum in the sea for an hour. <u>They've just left</u> / They've just been leaving.

j) Father <u>has left</u> / has been leaving the flat.

ENGLISH GRAMMAR PRACTICE

4. Choose the perfect continuation for the conversations below:

1. Where have you been?

    a) I've looked for you everywhere!

    b) I've been looking for you everywhere!

2. I'm sorry I'm late. Have you been waiting for long?

    a) I've waited for fifteen minutes!

    b) I've been waiting for fifteen minutes!

3. Has he already come?

    a) Yes, he has. He's been watching TV since he came.

    b) Yes, he has. He watched TV since he came.

4. I'm here now. What have you done so far?

    a) I've eaten my lunch. Now, I'm watching a film.

    b) I've been eating my lunch. Now, I'm watching a film.

5. She's left since noon. What do you think she's doing?

    a) She's driving. She's been driving for a long time.

    b) She's driving. She has driven for a long time.

6. Where's Jack?

    a) He's in the bathroom. He's having a bath. He's been having a bath for ten minutes already.

    b) He's in the bathroom. He's having a bath. He's had a bath since twenty minutes.

7. Has the plane landed already? Where's Ann?

a) Yes, it has. Ann's clearing customs. She's cleared customs for five minutes.

b) Yes, it has. Ann's clearing customs. She's been clearing customs for five minutes.

8. What's happened?

a) The car has stopped. We've been arriving at Aunt Jane's place.

b) The car has stopped. We've arrived at Aunt Jane's place.

9. Have you finished the book already?

a) No, I haven't. I'm still reading it. I've read it for the last three hours.

b) No, I haven't. I'm still reading it. I've been reading for the last three hours.

10. Where's my sweater?

a) Doris has taken it. She's been wearing it for three days.

b) Doris has taken it. She's worn it for three days.

5. Rephrase the sentences so that they contain the words given. Do not change the words and keep the meaning of the first sentence given:

a) They got married twenty years ago. (**BEEN**)
b) She started to listen to the news ten minutes ago. (**BEEN**)
c) The baby is crying. It started crying five minutes ago. (**FOR**)
d) They started taking driving lessons two weeks ago. (**BEEN**)
e) They came to work in this factory five years ago and they are still here. (**FOR**)
f) She started reading the reports an hour ago. (**BEEN**)
g) She came to stay with her cousin two days ago. (**STAYING**)
h) They left Bucharest by car an hour ago and they are going to Constantza. (**DRIVING**)
i) She's in the garden and she started watering the flowers half an hour ago. (**FOR**)
j) They went to walk in the park half an hour ago. (**BEEN**)

ENGLISH GRAMMAR PRACTICE

6. *Choose the most suitable word or phrase:*

1. What exactly_____?
    a) does he work   b) is he working

2. Why is he in bed? He is in bed because he _____ flu.
    a) catches   b) has caught   c) is catching

3. _____ that car? It's red.
a) are you seeing   b) have you seen   c) do you see

4. It's getting dark. What _____ now?
a) do you do   b) are you doing   c) have you been doing

5. She's sleeping. She _____ for five hours.
    a) sleeps   b) is sleeping   c) has been sleeping

6. The sun _____ right now. It's in the sky.
    a) has risen   b) rises   c) is rising

7. They _____ enough and they cannot pass the exam.
a) haven't learnt   b) aren't learning   c) learn

8. Who _____ to?
a) does this car belong   b) is belonging   c) has belonged

9. She _____ so far. We're still waiting for her.
a) doesn't come   b) isn't coming   c) hasn't come

ENGLISH GRAMMAR PRACTICE

10) What's he doing? He's writing. He _____ for ten minutes.

a) is writing   b) writes   c) has been writing   d) has written

7. Complete the second sentence so that it has the same meaning as the first sentence:

a) She keeps saying stupid things.

   She's _____ .

b) He prefers to stay at home.

   He does not _____ out.

c) She is staring at him.

   She is _____ insistently.

d) It doesn't matter his opinion, do it!

   Never mind _____, do it!

e) What is going on?

   What is _____?

f) I'm feeling run down.

   I'm quite _____.

g) Do you know the length of this road?

   How much _____?

h) What about having lunch in town today?

   What do you _____?

i) I'm not thinking of any day off because I have a lot of work to do.

   I am too _____ a day off.

j) He's going to the beach in order to sail for a few hours.

   He's _____ for a few hours.

ENGLISH GRAMMAR PRACTICE

8. Rewrite each sentence so that it contains the word given. Do not change the word and pay attention that the meaning of the second sentence is the same with the first sentence:

a) She is delivering a new lesson. (**TEACHING**)
b) They are forever asking questions! (**KEEP**)
c) Has he arrived already? (**IS**)
d) They have already left so you can't speak to them. (**AREN'T**)
e) The bus isn't the bus station anymore. (**LEFT**)
f) They don't have their bags anymore. (**LOST**)
g) She started singing an hour ago and she's still doing it. (**BEEN**)
h) George has just closed the door behind him. (**GOT**)
i) Mary is not here. She is in town. (**GONE**)
j) The bus leaves at one o'clock. (**DEPARTURE**)

ENGLISH GRAMMAR PRACTICE

9. Correct the errors:

   a) John has came in town already.
   b) He knows them since ages.
   c) They are studing for that test at the hour.
   d) She is always do that.
   e) She comes here before.
   f) They looks for the cat right now.
   g) They're wanting to make a trip to Budapest.
   h) He looks for his dog. He's been looking for it for five hours.
   i) It's a mess! We've just moving furniture around.
   j) He's liking that movie a lot.

10. Choose the most appropriate word or phrase from the list and complete the sentences below:

So far, until, early, last year, at, just, lately, recently, no sooner, normally

   a) They hadn't eaten anything _____ I came home.
   b) We _____ write to them once a month.
   c) They usually get up _____ because they don't like to be late.
   d) He had _____ got off the bike than the car hit him.
   e) They met in that resort _____.
   f) _____ she's read every new book in that bookshop.

g) They haven't seen each other too much _____.
h) She left the house _____ nine a.m.
i) We've _____ posted the letters for our friends.
j) They've bought their new house _____.

UNIT 13: FUTURE

EXPLANATIONS

We may express future using more tenses, depending on various situations.

SIMPLE FUTURE

Simple Future expresses:

1. A prediction, what we think it will happen in the future ➔ a time expression is normally present in the sentence

Ex: It will rain *tomorrow*.

2. Incertitude ➔ PERHAPS is present in the sentence

Ex: *Perhaps* he will come.

3. Probability, something almost sure ➔ PROBABLY is present in the sentence

Ex: It will *probably* work.

4. Certainty ➔ DEFINITELY is part of the sentence

Ex: I'll *definitely* do it.

5. We use simple future to express an action in the future when we have a clause whose action takes place in the future and it is introduced by when or if

Ex: I will come when she asks me to.

Ex: I will come if she asks me to.

6. We use simple future in the following constructions as well:

Subject + will + inf. + when + present perfect
Subject + will + inf. + as soon as + present perfect
Subject + will + inf. + after + present perfect

➔ to express that a future action will take place after another action in the future (in the clause sentence) has already taken place

NOTE: the order of the sentences does not matter

Ex: He will come to us after he has finished his work for the day.

Ex: As soon as he has finished his report, he'll deliver it.

Conjugation

Generally, in conjugation we use **WILL** (especially in casual language) for all persons. We may use **SHALL** for the first person singular and plural, but, usually, **SHALL** is used to express an offer, a request etc.

⇨ **WILL** ➔ in casual language – short form **'ll**
⇨ **SHALL** ➔ in formal language
⇨ **WILL**

    a) A promise: *I'll do it!*
    b) A threat: *You'll see what happens!*
    c) A greeting form: *I'll see you soon!*
    d) A decision made in the spur of the moment: *What can I do now? I know! I'll sew something.*
    e) A request: *Will you do it for me?*

⇨ **SHALL**

a) An offer: *Shall I take it for you?*

b) A suggestion: *Shall we have lunch in town?*

1. **Affirmative**

    Subject + will + bare inf.

2. **Negative**

    Subject + will not + bare inf.

    Subject + won't + bare inf.

3. **Interrogative**

    Will + subject + bare inf.?

4. **Interrogative – Negative**

    Will + subject + not + bare inf.?

    Won't + subject + bare inf.?

Note: *In spoken language, but not only, the short form* **WON'T** *is preferred to* **WILL NOT**.

TO BE GOING TO (NEAR FUTURE)

- *Plan, intention* ➔ Ex: I'm going to work on it.
- *Prediction concerning something we can see or about which we know something* ➔ Ex: Look! He's going to fall on the stairs!
- *May be used instead of present continuous (**however, we cannot use present continuous tense instead of near future – the meaning would be changed**)*

    ➔ Ex: I'm going to drive to the mountain. (*future plan*)

    ➔ Ex: I'm driving to the mountain. (*moment of speech*)

WILL or GOING TO?

WILL ➔ *in formal language or show a promise:*
   Ex: I'll learn that.
GOING TO ➔ *a decision (as in a plan), in usual language:*
   Ex: I'm going to learn that.

Note: **TO BE** *may be used both with* **WILL** *and* **TO BE GOING TO**:

WILL + TO BE ➔ Ex: I'll be back tomorrow.

TO BE GOING TO + TO BE ➔ Ex: I'm going to be back tomorrow.

Conjugation:

Affirmative:

   Subject + to be (present) + going + to-infinitive

   Ex: He's going to come back next week.

Negative:

   Subject + to be (present negative) + going + to-infinitive

   Ex: He isn't going to come back next week.

Interrogative:

   To be (present) + subject + + going + to-infinitive

   Ex: Are you going to take that job?

Interrogative – Negative:

   To be (present negative) + subject + + going + to-infinitive

   Ex: Aren't they going to come back for her birthday?

FUTURE CONTINUOUS

Future continuous expresses:

⇨ *A temporary action or situation in the future*

→ He'<u>ll be giving</u> a lecture *at three tomorrow*.

→ She'<u>ll be listening</u> to the radio *while* he's fixing the car tomorrow afternoon.

⇨ *Used to show that something happens because an arrangement has been made*

→ Ex: He'<u>ll be attending</u> the party. *He said so.*

Conjugation

NOTE: *It's a continuous aspect of a tense, therefore, we have to use* **TO BE + [VB+-ING].**

→ **TO BE** *will be in the future*

Affirmative:

Subject + will be + [vb.+-ING]

Ex: I'll be watching that documentary at six tomorrow evening.

Negative:

Subject + will not be + [vb.+-ING]

Subject + won't be + [vb.+-ING]

Ex: He won't be listening to you!

Interrogative:

Will + subject + be + [vb.+-ING]?

Ex: Will he be working at noon tomorrow?

Interrogative – Negative:

Will + subject + not+ be + [vb.+-ING]?

Won't + subject + be + [vb.+-ING]?

Ex: Won't he be having lunch at that time?

FUTURE PERFECT

Future perfect expresses an action that has not taken place yet, but it will, before a certain moment or before a certain action in the future

➔ *it is generally found in the main sentence*

Time expressions used with future perfect:
By, by the time, in x days / weeks / years etc.

Conjugation:
It is a perfect time ➔ *to have (in the future) + third form of the verb*

Affirmative:

Subject + will + have + 3rd form

Ex: I will have finished by three.

Negative:

Subject + won't + have + 3rd form

Ex: I won't have finished by then.

Interrogative:

Will + subject + have + 3rd form

Ex: Will they have arrived by six?

Interrogative – Negative:

Won't + subject + have + 3rd form

Ex: Won't they have finished by the time she comes?

FUTURE IN THE PAST

Future in the past expresses an action that takes place after an action in the past ➔ *used in clause sentence*

Conjugation:

➔ ***it is a future tense*** ➔ ***we use the auxiliary WILL + infinitive***

➔ ***it is a past tense*** ➔ ***WILL is in the past*** ➔ ***WOULD***

Conjugation:

Affirmative: subject + would + infinitive

　　Ex: He said he would come.

Negative: subject + wouldn't + infinitive

　　Ex: He said he wouldn't come.

UNIT 14: PRACTICE FUTURE - 1

1. Say what these people decide to do:

a) Have you ironed the clothes, Jane? – Oh, no, I have forgotten. I _____ them now.

b) Have you done your report, John? – No, I _____ it now.

c) Have you watered the flowers, Alice? – Oh, I've forgotten! I _____ now.

d) Have you brought some bread? – No, I haven't had time. I _____ now.

e) Have you woken John up? – No, not yet, I _____ now.

f) What else can we do now? – I know, we _____ to a movie.

g) I'm really tired and I can't wait for the bus again! I _____ a cab.

h) I have finished my work for today. What can I do now? I know, I _____ TV.

i) Have you bought the tickets for the film, dear? – No, I _____ two tickets right now.

j) I'm hungry. I don't know what to eat. – Hmm! I _____ some sandwiches.

ENGLISH GRAMMAR PRACTICE

2. Say what these people have already decided to do:

   a) They _____ (leave) on a trip next week.
   b) She _____ (come) to us on Thursday.
   c) They _____ (have) a meeting on Monday.
   d) I _____ (cook) a good meal on Sunday.
   e) You _____ (study) English this semester, as I can see.
   f) He _____ (take) a dog, I hear.
   g) I'm afraid they _____ (move) into another town.
   h) She _____ (get) married next year.
   i) John _____ (leave) the country this summer.
   j) I _____ (attend) the university this year.

3. Complete the sentences using **WILL** or **GOING TO**:

   a) Don't do that! You _____ stick yourself.
   b) Come with us! We _____ take a trip to the mountains next week.
   c) She _____ come on time, you _____ see.
   d) Look out! You _____ fall!
   e) It's ringing at the door. It _____ be John, I think.
   f) Oh, you have done it! What _____ they _____ say?

g) They sky is quite black. It _____ rain.

h) Our team _____ win the match.

i) My throat is sour. I _____ be sick.

j) She has bought a car. She _____ take driving lessons.

4. *There are some mistakes in the following sentences. Find them!*

a) They are meeting at noon tomorrow.
b) I think it's raining in a few minutes.
c) She's visiting friends every weekend.
d) It is probably raining tomorrow.
e) I'm going to fall! Help me!
f) Who is winning the next match?
g) Perhaps I'm coming to you tomorrow.
h) They will come next week, you'll see.
i) What time is she coming tomorrow?
j) I will probably call on you.

ENGLISH GRAMMAR PRACTICE

5. Choose the correct continuation of the conversations below:

a) Don't do that!
   1) You'll hurt yourself!
   2) You are going to hurt yourself!

b) You can't go out!
   1) It will rain.
   2) It's going to rain.

c) Why don't you buy a new coat?
   1) You will look smarter.
   2) You're going to look smarter.

d) Why do you want to sell your house?
   1) I'll move to London next month.
   2) I'm going to move to London next month.

e) Have you listened to the radio? What's the weather forecast for tomorrow?
   1) It will snow tomorrow.
   2) It's going to snow tomorrow.

f) Her mother is bringing her a cat tomorrow.
   1) How will she call it?
   2) How is she going to call it?

g) I've decided to buy a car.
  1) When will you buy it?
  2) When are you going to buy it?

h) She doesn't know what to cook tonight.
  1) I think she'll cook some spaghetti.
  2) I think she's going to cook some spaghetti.

i) I predict a score 2 – 4.
  1) I think it will be 1 – 2.
  2) It's going to be 1 – 2.

j) What about meeting at the cinema at three o'clock tomorrow afternoon?
  1) I'll be there.
  2) I'm going to be there.

6. Put the following sentences into the form requested in the brackets:

  a) She's going to come tomorrow evening. (**negative**)
  b) I'll be here at noon. (**negative**)
  c) It will snow tomorrow. (**question**)
  d) Sheila's going to go to the sea next summer. (**question**)
  e) Our team will win. (**question**)
  f) We are going to leave at noon. (**negative**)
  g) I'm going to move out next week. (**negative**)
  h) They won't win, I'm sure. (**affirmative**)

i) They'll come back soon. (**question**)
j) Perhaps he'll come. (**negative**)

7. *Choose the correct phrase underlined:*
   a) She will come / is going to come, you'll see / you are going to see.
   b) Let's go! The plane will take off / is going to take off soon.
   c) Go to that show! You will enjoy it / are going to enjoy it.
   d) He has bought a car because he will take / he is going to take driving lessons.
   e) I haven't found my geography book. – I will lend / I am going to lend you one.
   f) Our class will take / is going to take a trip to Spain.
   g) When will you be / are you going to be home?
   h) John doesn't think he will be / is going to be back at five.
   i) Why is he going out now? – He will buy / is going to buy a newspaper.
   j) I've missed the train. – What will you do / are you going to do now?

8. Choose the correct sentence in each mini – dialogue:

a) Can you come to my party tomorrow evening?

    1. Sorry, I'll go to the mountains.

    2. Sorry, I'm going to the mountains.

b) What have you planned for tomorrow?

    1. I'll play volleyball with my friends.

    2. I'm going to play volleyball with my friends.

c) What do you think the weather forecast for tomorrow is?

    1. I think it will rain tomorrow.

    2. I think it is going to rain tomorrow.

d) Answer the phone, please. Who do you think it is?

    1. It will be Mary. She must call me.

    2. It is going to be Mary. She must call me.

e) What do you say about meeting me at the café at seven tomorrow evening?

    1. I'll be there.

    2. I'm going to be there.

f) Mary is going to college next year.

    1. Really? What specialization will she take?

    2. Really? What specialization is she going to take?

g) It would be nice to meet all of us on Sunday next week.
   1. What will you do then?
   2. What are you going to do then?

h) I've seen the new film in town. You should go too.
   1. You will like it.
   2. You are going to like it.

i) There is a match between our team and theirs tomorrow.
   1. What will the score be?
   2. What is the score going to be?

9. *Put the verb given into a form of simple future, near future or present continuous. More than one answer may be possible*

   a) They _____ (leave) tomorrow morning. They have already bought the tickets.
   b) Sheila has finished lunch and she is thinking what to do. She decides that she _____ (read) a book.
   c) What _____ (they, do) on Saturday? – They _____ (go) to the cinema.
   d) When do you think you _____ (come) to me? – I don't know for sure. Perhaps I _____ (come) on Sunday afternoon.
   e) What's the weather like tomorrow night? – I hear it _____ (snow).

f) What _____ (they, do) next week? – They _____ (visit) their aunt.

g) Has he written to her so far? – No, but he _____ (probably, write) to her tomorrow.

h) Your sister _____ (go) to the disco on Friday evening. _____ (you, accompany) her?

i) Has he already left? – No, he _____ (fly) to Paris next week.

j) Have they already come back from their vacation? – No, but they _____ (probably, come) back next week.

10. Complete the second sentence so that it has a similar meaning to the first sentence:

a) She predicts a victory for our class in the competition.
   She thinks _____.
b) They have planned to go to a show tomorrow.
   They are _____.
c) She thinks of calling them up now.
   She will _____.
d) I decide to go there too.
   I'll _____.
e) They have decided to move out.
   They are _____.
f) John's party is on Friday.
   John is _____.
g) They intend to come back next weekend.
   They are _____.

h) What are your arrangements for the holiday?
   Where _____.
i) Okay! Meet me outside the cinema at four.
   Okay! I _____.
j) They don't plan to change schools after all.
   They aren't _____.

ENGLISH GRAMMAR PRACTICE

UNIT 15: PRACTICE FUTURE - 2

1. Put the verbs given into a form of simple future, near future or present continuous:

a) They _____ (listen) to you. Trust me!

b) Stephen _____ (go) to the sea on Friday.

c) We _____ (probably, think) of them at the time.

d) Maybe they _____ (do) those reports tomorrow.

e) What _____ (they, do) over the weekend? They _____ (ride) their bikes.

f) The exam is on Wednesday morning. – I _____ (be) there.

g) I decide she _____ (come) with us and that's it.

h) He has gone out. He _____ (play) football with his friends.

i) The train _____ (arrive) on time, believe me.

j) I think she _____ (not recover) too soon.

ENGLISH GRAMMAR PRACTICE

2. Correct the errors in these sentences. Some of them may be correct:

a) She is probably coming later so don't wait for her.
b) He will go out of the house soon, so come fast.
c) He will buy a bike next week. He will ride it to school.
d) What can I do now? I know! I'm going to read a book.
e) I've planned to go on a vacation. I'll leave next week.
f) It is snowing tomorrow so put something warmer on.
g) I'll come to you next week if you want.
h) They are talking about that incident when they'll meet.
i) I've listened to the radio and find out about that show. I'll go to see it.
j) Hurry up! The train will leave.

3. Choose the correct word or phrase underlined in each sentence:

a) Mary is coming / will come home when her husband will call / calls her.
b) They will clean / will be cleaning the house while the girls will cook / are cooking.
c) Please, wait quietly until he will call / calls you in.
d) I will have left / will be leaving for the sea at noon tomorrow.
e) I hope she will come / will be coming soon.

f) They have planned to go there. They will leave / are going to leave tomorrow.

g) What will you do / will you be doing in ten years' time?

h) After they will give / give us the information, we will go / will be going there.

i) Stop doing that! I'll punish you / I'm going to punish you otherwise.

j) She will come / will be coming with us as soon as she will hear / has heard we've booked the tickets.

ENGLISH GRAMMAR PRACTICE

4. Complete each part sentence a) to j) with one of the part sentences 1) to 10). Use each part sentence only once:

   a) You'll leave there _____
   b) In a few moments _____
   c) We'll start working on this project _____
   d) I'll tell that to my mother _____
   e) Go and buy tickets _____
   f) Kelly will cook dinner _____
   g) Next week at this time _____
   h) When I see him, _____
   i) In ten years, _____
   j) He said _____

   1) as soon as the committee has agreed with the plan
   2) she'll have retired from work
   3) when she comes back from work
   4) he'll have finished his test
   5) he could come next week
   6) I'll ask him to phone you
   7) after she washes her hands
   8) as soon as you have finished here
   9) we'll be swimming in the ocean
   10)   after the bus comes

ENGLISH GRAMMAR PRACTICE

5. Rewrite each sentence with **will / shall** or **going to**, using the verb underlined:

   a) How do you feel about <u>going</u> to the beach?
   b) She hopes <u>to be</u> back soon.
   c) They have planned <u>to write</u> the report in the afternoon.
   d) I'd like you <u>to cook</u> for me tonight.
   e) She has decided <u>to attend</u> that course.
   f) What about <u>buying</u> tickets for the theatre?
   g) They promise <u>not to be</u> late.
   h) Could I <u>do</u> that for you?
   i) I think I could <u>drink</u> some coffee.
   j) Can you <u>open</u> the door for me, please?

6. Correct the inappropriate verb forms. Not all the verb forms are inappropriate:

   a) By the time I come back, they will leave.
   b) After he will check the report, he will change his mind, you'll see.
   c) They won't come back until you will call them.
   d) Will he have lain in bed at this hour tomorrow?
   e) When the child will come back, I'll call you back.
   f) As soon as we will finish our work in the house, we will call on you.
   g) I'll be seeing Mary tomorrow so I can tell her about your party.

h) After the lecture will end, they will be going to the theatre.

i) He will be going to bed by the time you will arrive.

j) Alice will go to work by car after she will have her car repaired.

7. *Complete the second sentence so that it has a similar meaning to the first sentence:*

a) My son will go out to play after he does his homework.

　　My son _____ when _____.

b) Sidney will manage to come to us when she has finished her work today.

　　As soon as _____.

c) What job will she have in ten years' time?

　　What will _____?

d) Mary intends to buy herself a new raincoat.

　　Mary is _____.

e) They have planned to invite their friends to their party next Sunday.

　　They are _____.

f) How about having a cheese sandwich?

　　Shall _____?

g) Mary, could you give me a hand here?

　　Mary, will _____?

h) Please, John, stay here until I come back.

　　Please, John, don't _____.

i) They refuse to help me with my essay.

　　They won't _____.

j) I will be there in no time.

　　I won't _____.

8. Choose the most appropriate words underlined:

a) Marian is going to leave / will leave next month.
b) She will play / will be playing the match of her life at ten tomorrow.
c) They are probably going to break up / will probably break up soon.
d) I expect they are going to win / will win in this confrontation.
e) She thinks they are going to come / will come by train tomorrow.
f) Will he work / Will he be working at noon tomorrow? I want to call him.
g) He will be just leaving / is just about to leave so hurry up if you want / will want to see him.
h) She thinks she can't work here anymore so she will resign / is about to resign.
i) The train will leave / is due to leave at nine.
j) He won't have won / won't win, I suppose. The contest must have been very difficult.

UNIT 16: FUTURE – PROGRESS TEST

1. *Put the verb in brackets into a suitable tense:*

a) There's someone at the back door. – That _____ (be) Mary. She usually comes at the back door.

b) We _____ (not be) late. The journey _____ (not take) more than two hours.

c) _____ (he, work) next week? I want to invite him with us at the cottage.

d) Don't come so late! I usually _____ (sleep) at the hour.

e) By the time she comes, I _____ (leave).

f) They have already packed. They _____ (take) the train very early in the morning.

g) By tonight, you _____ (decide), won't you?

h) She has put the tomatoes in the pan. What _____ (she, do) next?

i) Please, call me as soon as you _____ (find) out the result of the test.

j) By this time next month, they _____ (arrive) in town.

ENGLISH GRAMMAR PRACTICE

2. Choose the most appropriate continuation for each sentence:

a) The train will be late even though _____
   1. it will come at ten
   2. it's due at ten
   3. it arrives at ten

b) According to the radio forecast _____
   1. it will rain tomorrow
   2. it's raining tomorrow
   3. It rains tomorrow

c) Hurry if you want to see Alice because _____
   1. she leaves
   2. she'll leave
   3. she's about to leave

d) I'll decide what I do after _____
   1. I will see him
   2. I see him
   3. I am seeing him

e) Mary will have written to him by the time _____
   1. he will come back
   2. he's coming back
   3. he comes back

f) In three months' time _____
   1. he'll be living here
   2. he lives here
   3. he's living here

g) Don't wait for him because _____
   1. he won't come
   2. he isn't coming
   3. he doesn't come

h) By the time Don arrives _____
   1. we'll have finished everything
   2. We've finished everything
   3. We finish everything

i) In two weeks, _____
   1. I'll work here
   2. I'll be working here
   3. I work here

j) As soon as I have got their answer, _____
   1. I'll let you know
   2. I let you know
   3. I'll have let you know

ENGLISH GRAMMAR PRACTICE

3. *Complete each sentence with a suitable word or phrase referring to future time:*

a) As soon as he _____ his new house, he will write to us about it.

b) Is _____ on Friday evening? I have tickets for that rock concert.

c) Wait for her until _____ her assignments if you want to go out with her.

d) When she is sixty, she _____ retire and move to the countryside to live there.

e) I've lost my wallet! How _____ a train ticket now?

f) They are _____ go to bed. You can't call them now.

g) She won't be long. She _____ taking her hat.

h) Don't worry, I _____ in touch with them next week.

i) You can call me then. I _____ to the news at the hour.

j) She _____ mad, if you call and ask.

ENGLISH GRAMMAR PRACTICE

4. Rewrite each sentence, beginning as shown, so that the meaning stays the same:

a) I don't think he has arrived in town.

   He won't _____.

b) The President expects the victory of his party.

   The President thinks that _____.

c) This house will take us at least one year to build.

   In two years' time at least, _____.

d) I've been learning French for ten years, come the end of the year.

   By the end of the year, I _____.

e) He won't be there until we come.

   By the time _____.

f) There will be a concert in town tomorrow evening.

   A concert _____.

g) I'll give you the book back when I have finished reading it.

   As soon as _____.

h) What about going to the theatre tomorrow?

   What do _____?

i) I need two years to complete this project.

   In two years _____.

j) Sheila will finish her work at the office first and then she'll come, probably.

   As soon as _____.

5. *Choose the most appropriate word or phrase underlined:*

   a) Andrew's sister will have left <u>by the time</u> / <u>when</u> we arrive.
   b) They will be having a meeting <u>at noon</u> / <u>by noon</u> tomorrow.
   c) There will not tests given <u>forthwith</u> / <u>from now on</u>.
   d) Mathias and I will come <u>by noon</u> / <u>at noon</u>, I promise.
   e) She'll be teaching <u>soon</u> / <u>now</u>.
   f) They won't have written to us <u>in a week</u> / <u>next week</u>.
   g) We are going to leave <u>at the end of the week</u> / <u>by the end of the week</u>.
   h) I'll be back <u>when</u> / <u>as soon as</u> the film starts.
   i) I can't come to you on Friday. I won't have finished everything <u>until then</u> / <u>then</u>.
   j) She'll be at home <u>after a few minutes</u> / <u>in a few minutes</u>.

6. Rewrite each sentence so that it contains the word in capitals. Do not change the word in any way:

a) She has to be here on time. (**WON'T**)
b) They are on the point of breaking relations with their neighbours. (**ABOUT**)
c) No one knows what she intends to do. (**GOING**)
d) They have their exams next month. (**TAKING**)
e) She won't have finished her domestic works by the time I come. (**UNTIL**)
f) Who will help you with your problem? (**GIVE**)
g) Tell her that she can see me in front of the post office when she comes. (**WILL**)
h) What have you planned for the weekend? (**TO**)
i) John will call you up when he finishes his projects. (**AFTER**)
j) Theodore is about to make a big mistake. (**OF**)

UNIT 17: CONDITIONAL TYPE 1, 2 AND 3 AND WISHES

EXPLANATIONS

CONDITIONAL SENTENCES

1. We can use it to describe an action that always takes place:

If + subject + simple present, subject + simple present

   Ex: If it snows a lot, the roads snow up.

2. We can use it to show what we must do in a certain situation:

If + simple present, imperative

   Ex: If it rains, take an umbrella.

CONDITIONAL TYPE I

Conditional type I ➔ expresses a real condition ➔ what happens in a real situation:

If + P.S. + will / won't

   Ex: If she comes, we'll go there.

We can also use:

   ➔ *Present continuous instead of present simple*

      Ex: If he's writing letters, I'll read something.

   ➔ *Present perfect instead of present simple*

      Ex: If I've read the book, I'll tell you.

Instead of IF we may use: UNLESS, PROVIDED, ON CONDITION

Ex: I will come unless I have to go there.

= I will come if I don't have to go there.

CONDITIONAL TYPE 2

→ *expresses an imaginary condition*
→ *expresses a thing that might happen*

Ex: I'd go to France if I had the money. (I'd = I would)

Note: in sentences after IF, we use present subjunctive that has a similar form with the simple past, but for the verb TO BE, where WERE is used for all persons

- *In spoken language, people use both WAS and WERE*
- *WOULD in spoken language is used in its short form:* **'d**
- *In usual language, IF may be replaced with:*
  IMAGINE, SUPPOSING

Ex: Imagine you knew everything about Maths. What would you do?

Ex: Supposing you were rich, what would you do?

→ ***IF I WERE YOU** – used for giving advice*

Ex: If I were you, I'd be more careful.

CONDITIONAL TYPE 3

Conditional type 3 ➔ *IF + PAST PERFECT + WOULD HAVE*

➔ *expresses an impossible condition; refers to things in the past*

Ex: If I had had a bike, I would have taken it on vacations.

Note: *We can eliminate IF by making the inversion **verb + subject***

Ex: Had I had a bike, I would have taken it on vacations.

➔ *BUT FOR – to show that something couldn't have happened without the help of something or someone*

Ex: But for you, I wouldn't have been able to do it.
Ex: But for his advice, she wouldn't have managed.

MODAL VERBS IN CONDITIONAL

MIGHT and COULD are often used in conditional to express incertitude

Observation: COULD may describe an ability too

In the conditional sentence the constructions with modal verbs are the following:

➔ *conditional type 1:*

MODAL VERB + INF. ➔ IN THE CONDITIONAL CLAUSE – PRESENT

Ex: If you are not careful, you might get a bad mark.

➔ *conditional type 2:*

MODAL VERB IN THE PAST + INF.

Ex: I could come if I had the time.

Ex: If I were attentive in class, I could be the first.

➔ *conditional type 3:*

MODAL VERB IN THE PAST + HAVE + 3ᴿᴰ FORM VERB

Ex: She might have come if she had had the time.

Had she had the time, she might have come.

If I had done my work, I could have got a better mark.

Had I done my work, I could have got a better mark.

WISHES

1) *about present* ➔ *similar to sentences in conditional type 2*

Ex: I wish I had a car. (= but I don't)

= If I had a car, I'd be happy.

2) *about the past* ➔ *similar to sentences in conditional type 3*

Ex: I wish I had paid attention in class. I'd know the lesson now.

= Had I paid attention in class, I'd have known the lesson.

= Had I paid attention in class, it would have been better for me.

3) WISHED + PAST PERFECT ➔ *wish about something in the past*

Ex: I wished I had a new house. (= but I don't have one)

4) with COULD ➔ *wish for a change you would like to do*

Ex: I wish I could come to you tomorrow

5) with HOPE ➔ *wish for the future*
HOPE + PRES. SIMPLE / WILL

Ex: I hope you will be here in time.

I hope you can do it.

6) IF ONLY ➔ *replaces WISH for emphasis*

Ex: If only I had a car. = I wish I had a car.

If only he didn't come. = I wish he didn't come.

UNIT 18: PRACTICE CONDITIONAL TYPE 1 AND 2

1. Choose the correct word or phrase underlined:

a) If they go / will go there with us, they see / will see that I was right.

b) If the rain stops / will stop, we go / we'll go for a walk.

c) I'll check the documents and if they are / will be all right, I join / will join your business.

d) If the wind blows / will blow, we aren't able / won't be able to climb up that hill.

e) If he tells / will tell the truth, then we are / will be in a serious trouble.

f) If they arrive / will arrive at home on time, they see / will see the movie with us.

g) If you read / will read this novel, you discover / will discover an interesting view on life.

h) I hope he won't do it again. If he breaks / will break the window again, Mr. Thompson gets angry / will get angry.

i) If they keep / will keep working like that, they reach / will reach bankruptcy, to be sure.

j) He comes / will come to visit you tomorrow, if you give / will give him a phone call and invite / will invite him.

ENGLISH GRAMMAR PRACTICE

2. Complete the sentences using the verbs given:

a) I'm not sure when I have told them to come to the cinema. What shall I do? – Don't worry, if they _____ (come) earlier, they _____ (wait) for us.

b) You say to a friend: An exhibition has just opened downtown. What do you say? Will you come with me? Your friend replies: If you _____ (invite) me to come, I _____ (join) you.

c) Oh, John, we are in a real trouble. Can you help us? – Don't worry, if I _____ (can) do something, I _____ (do) it.

d) You meet a friend you haven't seen for a long time and you say: If you _____ (want), I _____ (invite) you to my house on Sunday evening.

e) This is a very interesting painting exhibition. If you _____ (not go) to see it, you _____ (regret).

f) You are with friends and find out that you have taken your exams. You say: _____ (you, excuse) me if I _____ (go) to send a telegram to my parents about my exams?

g) A friend tells you that he doesn't know what happened with some common friends. You reply: Don't worry, if I _____ (talk) to them, they _____ (tell) me everything.

ENGLISH GRAMMAR PRACTICE

h) I want to ask Mark to help me with this problem. If he _____ (do) me this favour, I _____ be grateful to him.

i) I can't work out the answer. Who can help me? – What _____ (you, say) if I _____ (tell) you that I know the answer?

j) I need your help in this matter. _____ (you, help) me if I _____ (ask) you?

3. Complete each sentence, using **IF**, **UNLESS** or **WOULD**:

a) We will go to a picnic tomorrow _____ it rains.

b) She _____ agree with you _____ you told her the truth.

c) I _____ build a house in town _____ I had the money.

d) She won't come to you _____ you invite her.

e) They _____ visit the Browns _____ they were invited.

f) She will go to hospital _____ she recovers.

g) No one of his brothers could take care of him _____ he got sick.

h) My brother _____ never forgive me _____ I spoke to his boss.

i) He _____ be calmer _____ he knew that he was right.

ENGLISH GRAMMAR PRACTICE

j) You _____ think like me _____ you knew the entire story.

4. Complete each sentence a) to j) with an ending from 1) to 10):

a) If you cared of your aunt, _____.
b) If I were sure I didn't bother you, _____.
c) His brother would laugh at me _____.
d) If your mother heard that, _____.
e) If I told you what I saw in their office a few days ago _____.
f) I couldn't add anything more _____.
g) If she talked to him about that, _____.
h) If someone saw her doing that stupid thing, _____.
i) I would be against your projects _____.
j) What would you do _____.

1) if he saw what I was doing.
2) you wouldn't believe me.
3) if I could have a word to say.
4) you wouldn't treat her with so lack of respect.
5) she would be very upset.
6) if I were to make the presentation.
7) if you had to make such a difficult decision?
8) I would tell you all the adventures we had during the summer holiday.
9) what would she say?
10) he would pretend he hadn't heard.

5. Choose the correct phrase underlined:

a) I spent / **would spend** a few days with you if I **had** / would have money.

b) I suppose he concludes / **will conclude** a contract with you if he **reads** / will read your project.

c) They **go** / will go swimming unless it **is** / will be cold.

d) If he told / **would tell** you about his trip, you didn't believe / **wouldn't believe** him.

e) I couldn't interfere between them even though I want / **wanted**.

f) He were / **would be** very disappointed if you **told** / would tell him the truth.

g) If I **told** / would tell him what I heard, our friendship broke / **would break**.

h) Paul were forced / **would be forced** to resign if his boss **found out** / would find out the truth about him.

i) If he **wants** / will want to marry her, he must tell her too.

j) If you **knew** / would know the truth about her, you didn't want / **wouldn't want** to be in touch with her anymore.

UNIT 19: PRACTICE CONDITIONAL TYPE 2 AND 3

1. *Choose the correct word or phrase underlined:*

a) She would be / would have been surprised if she heard / had heard that story. She couldn't believe / couldn't have believed her eyes.

b) I would punish / would have punished you for these words if I were / had been your mother.

c) They would leave / would have left in due time if they woke up / had woken up early the other day.

d) Shirley would come / would have come to visit you if you invited / had invited her, to be sure.

e) If you told / tell that to Peter, he would be / would have been very happy, you know.

f) I suppose he would eat / would have eaten if you told / had told him that Mary was the cook. He likes her cooking. It's a pity you didn't do it!

g) Do you think they would do it / would have done it if they saw / had seen the plans? Then, why didn't you show them the plans?

h) Don't be silly! Of course I would do / would have done it if I had time.

i) You know, if I had / had had time, I would take / would have taken driving lessons. Maybe next month I'll find the time.

j) She didn't come! – Yes, I know. If she <u>had</u> / <u>had had</u> the means, she <u>would come</u> / <u>would have come</u>.

2. Rewrite each comment beginning as shown:

a) Imagine you could drive! What would you do?
   What _____ if _____?
b) I think you should try it.
   If _____.
c) Why doesn't she learn more? That's what I'd do.
   If _____.
d) I think you should practice more.
   If I _____.
e) I think you should call him if he has problems.
   If I _____.
f) Imagine you do that! What would Ellen say?
   If you _____, _____?
g) I think you should change your behaviour. That's what I'd do.
   If _____.
h) Why don't you go there and see with your own eyes? That's what I'd do.
   If _____.
i) I think it will rain tomorrow. Then I'll take the car.
   If _____.
j) Imagine she brings you the gift you expect. How would you feel?
   How _____ if _____?

3. Choose the correct word or phrase underlined in each sentence:

a) If I <u>dared</u> / <u>had dared</u>, I <u>would address</u> / <u>would have addressed</u> you this question. Would you answer me?

b) I <u>would understand</u> / <u>would have understood</u> better his deeds if I <u>knew</u> / I <u>had known</u> the circumstances, but he didn't tell me anything.

c) If I <u>weren't</u> / <u>hadn't been</u> too tired, I <u>would show you off</u> / <u>would have shown you off</u>, but I want to go to bed now.

d) I <u>would spend</u> / <u>would have spent</u> a few days with them if I <u>had</u> / <u>had had</u> vacation but unfortunately, I had to go to work.

e) Your students <u>would be</u> / <u>would have been</u> very amazed if you <u>told</u> / <u>had told</u> them about your research. You haven't told them so far, have you?

f) She <u>wouldn't go</u> / <u>wouldn't have gone</u> there if she <u>didn't hear</u> / <u>hadn't heard</u> that he was going to be there. That's why she came.

g) Marilee <u>wouldn't leave</u> / <u>wouldn't have left</u> there hadn't she got their invitation.

h) <u>I wouldn't buy</u> / <u>I wouldn't have bought</u> bread if I <u>knew</u> / <u>had known</u> that you also bought some.

i) Maria <u>would write</u> / <u>would have written</u> to you if she <u>knew</u> / <u>had known</u> your address but she asked me about it only a few days ago.

j) The boy <u>wouldn't go swimming</u> / <u>wouldn't have gone swimming</u> if his mother <u>didn't allow</u> / <u>hadn't allowed</u> him to go, but she did.

4. Rephrase the sentences using what is already given. Keep the meaning of the first sentence:

a) I didn't wake up early and I was late for school.

    If I _____, I _____.

b) Mary didn't buy tickets in due time and therefore she couldn't go to the show.

    If Mary _____.

c) Alice and I left too late and therefore we didn't manage to get there on time.

    If Alice and I _____.

d) They didn't buy anything to eat in their way home and they couldn't cook dinner.

    Had _____.

e) Alice didn't do her homework and she got a bad mark.

    Had _____.

f) We could leave early and therefore we could get to the airport on time.

    If we _____.

g) Maria didn't catch the last bus and she had to take a cab.

    If Maria _____.

h) Alison and John didn't agree with that matter and therefore they broke up.

    Had _____.

i) You didn't eat anything and that's why you feel so unwell.

    Had _____.

j) The boys were punished because they had fought in the schoolyard.

    Hadn't _____.

ENGLISH GRAMMAR PRACTICE

5. Correct the errors in the following sentences. Some of them may be correct:

a) This is a good play. You would like it if you had seen it.

b) If you asked me to come with you, I would have refused you, and you know it.

c) I doubt he would feel the same about her if she tells him her secret.

d) What would they have believed about me if I did it?

e) Your father would have got mad if he heard what you did.

f) Would you do it if you had been asked to do it one day?

g) If Ann would ask you to give her these books for a while, would you do it?

h) If she asked him to help her with her suitcases, would he have done it?

i) If you had some spare time, what would you have done?

j) He wouldn't be in this situation if he had listened to his father's advice, but he hadn't.

UNIT 20: PRACTICE WISHES

1. *Choose the correct word or phrase underlined:*

a) I wish I spend / spent a few days in the mountains. I'm too tired.

b) He wished he had / had had a house in this neighbourhood. It is very quiet.

c) She wishes she left / had left early. She wouldn't have been late.

d) They wish they manage / could manage but they couldn't.

e) I wished I lived / had lived in the country. It would have been more peaceful.

f) They boy wishes he has / had such a toy car but he doesn't.

g) She wishes she learnt / had learnt more because now she'd have been at the university.

h) My aunt wished she went / had gone to France last year but she had no money.

i) Lauren wishes she buys / bought a car. Maybe next year she'll have the money.

j) The teachers wish their students studied / had studied more but they don't do it.

2. Choose the correct continuation for each sentence:

a) I am very tired and I'd like to go to bed but I haven't finished my homework.
    1. I wish I had gone to bed.
    2. I wish I could go to bed.

b) She is very upset because of her son.
    1. She wishes he learnt more.
    2. She wishes he learns more.

c) I left too late for work yesterday and I got into big trouble.
    1. I wish I left earlier.
    2. I wish I had left earlier.

d) The woman is very sick now and she can't do anything.
    1. She wishes she went to the doctor sooner.
    2. She wishes she had gone to the doctor sooner.

e) The little boy lost his toys yesterday and now he regrets.
    1. He wishes he were more attentive.
    2. He wishes he had been more attentive.

f) The man was too tired and therefore he made an accident.

    1. Now he wishes he didn't drive and stayed at home.

    2. Now he wishes he hadn't driven and he had stayed at home.

g) She did very poor in her test yesterday.

    1. She wishes she studied more.

    2. She wishes she had studied more.

h) Alice is heartbroken now.

    1. She wishes she didn't break up with David.

    2. She wishes she hadn't broken up with David.

i) Edward and John went to the movies yesterday and missed Ann's visit.

    1. They wish they stayed home instead.

    2. They wish they had stayed home instead.

j) We missed the train in the morning and we had to wait for the next one.

    1. We wish we didn't waste so much time at breakfast.

    2. We wish we hadn't wasted so much time at breakfast.

ENGLISH GRAMMAR PRACTICE

3. Complete each sentence in a suitable way:

a) I'm thirsty. If only _____ a bottle of mineral water.

b) She is too tired. If only she _____ more last night.

c) She is too fat now. If only she _____ so much.

d) They are very sad now. If only _____ because of that stupid thing and _____ up. Now they would have still been together.

e) She wishes she _____ that dress. It was a waste of money.

f) The teacher wishes he _____ the trip to the mountain because his students _____ a lot of stupid things.

g) If only I _____ the answer to his question. Maybe I would have solved the entire situation.

h) If only maths _____ so difficult. Maybe I would have better marks.

i) He hopes he _____ better in his next test. This one was a real mess.

j) She hopes he _____ tomorrow. She really needs his help.

ENGLISH GRAMMAR PRACTICE

4. Correct the errors in the following sentences. Some of them may be correct:

a) I wish I had more time to work on this project but I didn't have enough time.
b) She wishes she will go to the mountains soon.
c) We wished we met them when we were in Berlin.
d) John wishes he has a new car.
e) They wish they were there last year too.
f) Donna and Trish wish they took a cab but they hadn't.
g) Lauren and I wish we visit them but we don't have the time.
h) They wish she came to their party but she left somewhere else.
i) They wished I lent them the book but I needed it too.
j) I wished I went to that play. I hear it is great.

UNIT 21: CONDITIONALS AND WISHES CONSOLIDATION

1. Rephrase each sentence, beginning as shown, and keep the meaning of the sentence:

a) Supposing you had enough time. What would you do?
   If _____.
b) Imagine you could go there. What would you take with you?
   What _____?
c) Why don't you do your work? That's what I'd do.
   If _____.
d) Supposing they had been willing to come! What would you say?
   What _____?
e) Imagine you had such a robot. What would you put it to do?
   What _____?
f) Imagine you could buy a trip to Paris. What would you say?
   If _____?
g) Why don't you buy yourself a dog? That's what I'd do.
   If _____.
h) Supposing you could solve all their problems. What would you do?
   If _____?

ENGLISH GRAMMAR PRACTICE

i) Imagine you were in his shoes. What would you do?

    If _____?

j) Supposing someone told you the same things to you. How would you feel?

    If _____?

2. *Choose the most suitable word or phrase underlined:*

   a) If I <u>was</u> / <u>were</u> you, I <u>would go</u> / <u>would have gone</u> to the beach.

   b) If they <u>had</u> / <u>had had</u> time, they <u>would go</u> / <u>would have gone</u> to the amusements park, but they hadn't.

   c) Unless it <u>doesn't rain</u> / <u>rains</u> / <u>will rain</u> / <u>won't rain</u>, I <u>will go</u> / <u>won't go</u> / <u>don't go</u> to the mountains with my friends.

   d) I <u>would buy</u> / <u>would have bought</u> a bike if I <u>had</u> / <u>had had</u> money, but I hadn't.

   e) The boy <u>wouldn't be late</u> / <u>wouldn't have been late</u> if he <u>woke up</u> / <u>had woken up</u> on time, but he woke up only at nine.

   f) You are not patient at all. If you <u>were</u> / <u>are</u>, you <u>might find out</u> / <u>find out</u> interesting things.

   g) If your son <u>had studied more</u> / <u>studied more</u>, he <u>could have been admitted</u> / <u>was admitted</u> in the university.

   h) You are broke again. If you <u>didn't spend</u> / <u>hadn't spent</u> so much, you <u>might have</u> / <u>might have had</u> some money left.

i) <u>Hadn't he been</u> / <u>weren't he</u> so distracted, he <u>might notice</u> / <u>might have noticed</u> she was actually looking and smiling at him.

j) <u>Hadn't it been</u> / <u>if it weren't</u> for her, they <u>wouldn't have</u> / <u>wouldn't have had</u> that chance.

3. Complete the sentences in accordance with the situations given:

a) He didn't buy any tickets, so we couldn't go to the movie.

    Had _____.

b) She missed the train, so she couldn't come with us.

    Hadn't _____.

c) They lost their way, so they didn't reach the chalet.

    Hadn't _____.

d) Shirley was upset with him, so she didn't go to meet him.

    Hadn't _____.

e) We were lazy, so we didn't help them at all.

    Hadn't _____.

f) You left in a hurry, so you didn't see her.

    Hadn't _____.

g) I lost my purse in town, so I couldn't buy anything for dinner.

    Hadn't _____.

h) She was absent-minded and she forgot to buy some bread and milk.

    Hadn't _____.

i) I didn't want to meet them so I told them I was out of town for a while.

ENGLISH GRAMMAR PRACTICE

Had _____.

j) Mark helped me a lot and that's why I succeeded in my project.

But for _____.

4. Choose the most suitable word or words underlined for each sentence:

a) I'm hungry now. I wish I ate / had eaten in the morning.

b) I'm not well. I wish I didn't drink / hadn't drunk so much syrup.

c) If only I had / had had a car. I could be there in time.

d) If only I hadn't read / didn't read so much! I have a migraine.

e) I hope I came / I will come to your anniversary.

f) I wish you saw / had seen that. It's fantastic!

g) I wish I had / had had a bigger house. I could have friends over.

h) But for them, she wouldn't have come / hadn't come.

i) Supposing they had a boat, we could have sailed / could sail in the Caribbean.

j) She wished she didn't sent that letter / she hadn't sent that letter.

5. Fill in with an appropriate word or with a phrase:

a) I'm very tired. I wish _____ a rest.
b) It is lovely here. I wish _____ a house here.
c) My stomach hurts. I wish _____ that sandwich.
d) It seems to be a lovely place. I hope _____ a lot of time here.
e) If only _____ so much. I've forgotten my umbrella and I'm wet.
f) This purse is a real piece of work. I wish _____ money to buy it.
g) They want to go there soon. If only _____ a few days off!
h) If only _____ money on me! That's a beautiful coat.
i) I have a terrible headache! If only my neighbours _____ the noise!
j) But for her intervention, he _____ the contract.

UNIT 22: MODAL VERBS

Explanations:
- *Generally, they do not change their form in conjugation depending on the person*
- *They do not use auxiliary verbs within the conjugation* ➔ *Exception:* **TO HAVE TO**

MODAL VERBS IN PRESENT

1. CAN, CAN'T, CANNOT (formal)

➔ *to show ability* ➔ *may be replaced with* **TO BE ABLE TO**

Ex: I can ride a horse.
Can she sing?

➔ *permission (informal)*

Ex: Can I go now?
I can't come to you. Mother doesn't agree with that.

2. MAY, MIGHT

➔ *permission* (formal)

Ex: May I open that window? It is very hot in here.
May I leave the table?

➔ *to show possibility or incertitude*

    Ex: He might get that job.

            I may / might come tonight.

3. MAY NOT, MIGHT NOT ➔ *shows incertitude*

    Ex: I may not come tomorrow. (= *but who knows, I might*)

4. COULD ➔ *incertitude* ➔ *used mainly with TO BE*

    Ex: I could be there in time. (= *but I don't think so*)

5. MUST, CAN'T ➔ *impossibility or certitude, it depends on its appearance*

    Ex: He must be in trouble. (*certitude*)

            He can't come tomorrow. (*impossibility*)

            She can't be there. (=*of course not*)

6. MUST, HAVE TO ➔ *compulsion, necessity*

    Ex: You must finish it.

            They have to come.

    HAVE TO ➔ *shows rules made by other people*

Observation: In informal language, we prefer to use HAVE GOT TO.

    Ex: You've got to do it.

    MUST ➔ *emphasizes the importance of an action*

    Ex: You must go there!

7. MUSTN'T ➔ *expresses the forbidden action*
   Ex: She mustn't go there.

8. DON'T HAVE TO ➔ *expresses something that it is not necessary*
   ➔ *similar to* **NEEDN'T**
   Ex: You don't have to take it.
         You needn't take it.

9. SHOULD / SHOULDN'T
   ➔ *expresses an opinion*
      Ex: I shouldn't do it if I were you.
   ➔ *often used for giving advice*
      Ex: I think you should try harder.
            I think they should have lower prices.
   ➔ *expresses an action that is expected*
      Ex: They should answer our letter next week.

10. OUGHT TO / OUGHT NOT TO
   ➔ *expresses the same situations as SHOULD / SHOULDN'T*
      Ex: I think you ought to come.
            = I think you should come.

11. HAD BETTER ('D BETTER)
   ➔ *has the meaning like SHOULD / OUGHT TO*
      Ex: I think you'd better try harder.

MODAL VERBS IN THE PAST

1. COULD / COULDN'T / WAS ABLE TO

➔ *express ability*

Note: TO BE ABLE TO *shows that something was possible and took place.*

Ex: I could drive a car when I was eighteen.
I was able to drive a car when I was eighteen.

2. MIGHT HAVE DONE / MAY HAVE DONE / COULD HAVE DONE (something)

Ex: I think he might have come back.

3. HAD TO / DIDN'T HAVE TO / DIDN'T NEED TO / NEEDN'T HAVE + VERB 3RD FORM

➔ *express compulsion*

Ex: When I was in school, I had to do my homework every day.

I needn't have read that material too.
(= I did something unnecessary)

4. SHOULD HAVE DONE / OUGHT TO HAVE DONE

➔ *They express advice or opinion, but generally, we use them to criticise an action*

Ex: You shouldn't have said that.

ENGLISH GRAMMAR PRACTICE

UNIT 23: PRACTICE MODAL VERBS

1. *Choose the correct word underlined:*

   a) I think he can / must / might come tomorrow.
   b) You might / must / had better leave soon. They're waiting.
   c) You might / should / can do your homework.
   d) That's not right. This may / can't / should be the answer.
   e) It's ringing at the door. It can / must / ought to be John.
   f) They left half an hour ago. They must / can / have to be there now.
   g) I can't / may not / mustn't go out. I have some work to do.
   h) You ought to / must / have to write it down. You'll forget it.
   i) You are crazy. You shouldn't / don't have to / can eat too much.
   j) Ann must / should / might be home now. She finishes work at five.

2. *Rewrite the sentences beginning as show and using a modal verb so that the meaning stays the same:*

a) John will probably come to your party.

   John _____.

b) We have a very severe teacher and we get bad marks if we don't do our homework.

   We _____.

c) They are in town now. It's possible that they'll come back at noon.

   They _____.

d) You will have stomach ache. You eat too much.

   You _____.

e) I'm sure Jill will not come to you because she's sick.

   Jill _____.

f) I bet he will do the work very well. He knows a lot about this subject.

   He _____.

g) She isn't allowed to go to the beach today. She's grounded.

   She _____.

h) The sun is too bright. You'll get sunburnt.

   You _____.

i) The child has played a lot. It think it's sleeping now.

   The child _____.

j) It is not necessary for you to do that too.

   You _____.

3. Rewrite the sentences so that they contain the word given and the meaning stays the same:

a) Alice will probably move out soon. (**MIGHT**)
b) It is not good to drink so much beer. (**SHOULDN'T**)
c) I think he has already come home. (**MUST**)
d) I've heard a car stopping in front of the house but they don't have a car. (**CAN'T**)
e) Smoking is bad for you. Give up smoking and you will feel better. (**HAD BETTER**)
f) I think it's too late for me. I'll be late for work. (**OUGHT TO**)
g) It is not necessary to write everything. (**NEEDN'T**)
h) It's possible that it will rain tomorrow. (**MAY**)
i) The meeting starts at ten. You are not allowed to be late. (**CAN'T**)
j) I'll go home because I have work to do. (**MUST**)

4. Fill in the blanks with a modal verb:

a) You _____ go there. You'll have a lot of trouble.
b) Children _____ go out without their parents.
c) He _____ learn this time because otherwise he'll fail again.
d) You _____ hurry. The bus will leave without you.
e) He _____ be here at midnight. – Yes, I think so.

f) I _____ done that stupid thing!

g) When he was a child, he _____ to do so much work.

h) You _____ forgotten it at home.

i) I think she _____ taken the train instead.

j) She _____ sung well when she was younger.

5. *Rewrite each sentence so that it contains the word given and the meaning stays the same:*

a) When I was at school, I was supposed to learn a lot. (**HAD**)

b) Oh, dear! What an idea! It was possible to fall! (**COULD**)

c) They didn't come yesterday. Probably they didn't finish their work. (**MIGHT**)

d) You're completely run down. Working so hard wasn't such a good idea. (**SHOULD**)

e) She can't find her book. Yesterday she had it but now it's gone. (**MUST**)

f) I didn't talk to him. The line was busy. (**COULDN'T**)

g) They didn't pass the exam. I think they didn't pay enough attention in class. (**MIGHT**)

h) She graduated the first. Probably she worked hard. (**MUST**)

i) I helped them with their furniture but they could have managed by themselves. (**NEEDN'T**)

j) He's not sure but he thinks that he left it at home. (**MIGHT**)

UNIT 24: PASSIVE VOICE

EXPLANATIONS

ACTIVE VOICE

→ ***SUBJECT DOES THE ACTION;***

→ ***THE ACTION IS REFLECTED ON THE OBJECT***

Ex: **The girl** is reading *a book*.

→ the girl = subject → executes the action

→ a book = direct object → the action reflects on it

PASSIVE VOICE

→ ***AN OBJECT (AGENT OBJECT) PERFORMS THE ACTION***

→ ***THE ACTION IS REFLECTED ON THE SUBJECT***

Ex: The book is read *by the girl.*

→ the book – subject → action is reflected on it

→ by the girl – agent object → does the action

NOTE: *Transitive verbs are the only verbs used in passive voice.*

- ***TRANSITIVE VB = verb with direct object***

Ex: She washes ***her clothes*** every day.

➜ *her clothes* – is the answer for the question: What does she wash every day? ➜ direct object

- **INTRANSITIVE VB** = *verb that cannot have a direct object*

   Ex: I go to office every morning.

Passive voice shows an action done by someone else than the subject.

➜ **The subject suffers the consequences of the action.**
➜ **The agent object executes the action.**

Characteristics:
➜ *formed with the auxiliary* **TO BE** *(conjugated in the tense of the sentence) + the past participle of the verb (3rd form of the verb)*
➜ *the direct object in the sentence in the active voice becomes the subject in the sentence in the passive voice*

Ex1: People read newspapers every day. (***active voice***)
       Newspapers are read every day. (***passive voice***)

Ex2: Someone broke the window. (***active voice***)
       The window was broken. (***passive voice***)

➜ *we use passive voice to emphasize a piece of information (see Ex.1)*
➜ *we use it in written form and in formal language*
➜ *when we include the information referring to who did the action, we use* **BY**

Ex: The window was broken **by our neighbour's son**.
by our neighbour's son = agent object

➔ *to show the tool with which the action is done, we use the preposition:* **WITH**

Ex: The window was broken **with the ball**.

Notes:
1) *It is not necessary to mention the agent*
2) *Usually, we use passive voice when:*

➔ *we don't know who did the action*

➔ *when it is not necessary to know who did the action*

➔ *when it is obvious who did the action*

Ex: The man was arrested. (*by police*)

Certain verbs have two objects:

BUY	OFFER	TAKE
GIVE	PROMISE	SEND
LEND	SELL	

➔ *In this case, we may build two sentences in passive voice, using each of these objects for subject.*

Ex: He promised her a bike.
(1) A bike was promised to her.
(2) She was promised a bike.

TO BE BORN – *It is a passive construction, however, it does not have that meaning*

Ex: He was born in Austria.

HAVE SOMETHING DONE

➔ *we use it to show that someone else does something for us*

Note the difference:

Ex 1: I cut my hair. (*I did it myself, with no help*)

Ex 2: I had my hair cut. (*someone else did it for me*)

➔ *we can also use it to express an unpleasant incident*

Ex: I had my car stolen.

We form Passive Voice with:

TO BE (in the necessary tense) + 3rd form of the verb

Ex: I **was told** about it yesterday.

Ex: The car **was vandalized** two days ago.

Ex: She **will be given** an answer soon.

Ex: They **will have been given** that book.

UNIT 25: PRACTICE PASSIVE VOICE

1. *Underline what is not necessary in the following sentences:*

   a) The boy was taught English at school by a teacher.
   b) The car was stolen by someone yesterday.
   c) He was fined in the street by a policeman.
   d) The meat was stolen by the cat.
   e) He was put some questions by someone.
   f) The fish was caught by a man.
   g) They were told to the teacher by their colleagues.
   h) The sink was fixed by a plumber.
   i) The car was bought by someone.
   j) She was injured by someone yesterday.

2. *Fill in the blanks with a verb in passive voice so that the meaning of the first sentence stays the same:*

a) They asked him about the new rules.
He _____ about the new rules.

b) She left her purse on the desk.
Her purse _____ on the desk.

c) The women bought new bags from that shop.
New bags _____ from that shop.

d) They dug the garden in the morning.
The garden _____ in the morning.

e) Eminescu wrote the great poem "The Morning Star".
The great poem "The Morning Star" _____ by Eminescu.

f) Columbus discovered America.
America _____ by Columbus.

g) British colonised a part of Africa.
A part of Africa _____ by British.

h) Russians defeated Napoleon during his campaign in the East.
Napoleon _____ during his campaign in the East by Russians.

i) Dogs chase cats.
Cats _____ by dogs.

j) The Sun warms up Earth.
Earth _____ by the Sun.

ENGLISH GRAMMAR PRACTICE

3. Correct the errors:

a) Nothing was deciding then.
b) They were hit with a car.
c) She sewed her dress by a needle.
d) We were being lost in the woods.
e) Houses are built in the neighbourhood now.
f) The students were examined when I came in.
g) The lights had turned off when I got there.
h) The dog will be taken to a walk at noon.
i) The work will have done by then.
j) The wild animals in the zoo will be feed soon.

4. Rewrite each sentence so that it contains the word in brackets. Don't change the words and keep the meaning of the first sentence:

a) They are painting our house tomorrow. (**HAVING**)
b) She has cut her hair. (**HAD**)
c) They mended our car yesterday. (**HAD**)
d) They have brought your furniture. (**HAD**)
e) The thieves stole her purse. (**HAD**)
f) The children broke her window the other day. (**HAD**)
g) They repaired my washing machine in the morning. (**HAD**)
h) Tomorrow, they'll take my child from school. (**HAVE**)
i) The professor will correct their exams tomorrow. (**HAVE**)
j) By noon tomorrow, they will have finished refurnishing my kitchen. (**HAD**)

5. Rewrite each sentence, beginning as show. The meaning must stay the same:

a) He was chosen member of the committee last year.

   He became _____.

b) She was asked by the person behind her if she was getting off at the next bus stop.

   The person _____.

c) They were required to do their projects by their boss.

   Their boss _____.

d) She was told to go there by her mother.

   Her mother _____.

e) I was appointed head of department last year.

   They appointed _____.

f) These books were written by some famous authors.

   Some famous authors _____.

g) She found the note left by her mother in which she was asked to do the plans for the vacation.

   Her mother _____.

h) The toys were arranged by the housekeeper in the child's room.

   The housekeeper _____.

i) Someone was here because I was left a note.

   Someone _____ me _____.

j) There was a meeting yesterday and he talked but he wasn't believed.

   No one present _____.

ENGLISH GRAMMAR PRACTICE

6. Correct the sentences below. Some of them may be correct:

a) They were said some awful stories and they are still scared.
b) He is asked a difficult question but he couldn't answer.
c) Mary asked her son to do that job and he did what he were told.
d) The report was completed two days ago.
e) Someone told her to go there and she went where she was told.
f) Someone are left you a package with the receptionist.
g) The bridge built a few years ago.
h) She thinks you are right because she was shown some evidence.
i) The garbage took outside an hour ago. Janine did it.
j) They were required to answer to all the questions on the paper.

UNIT 26: REPORTED SPEECH

EXPLANATIONS

Definition: it is reported speech when someone's words are reported.

Characteristics:

→ if a sentence is put into reported speech close to the moment of the statement, nothing changes in the sentence

Ex: He's on the phone. **He says he's coming to us.**

→ usually, reported speech is shown using a verb in the past and optionally **THAT**

Changes when putting a statement in reported speech:

1) *simple present* → *simple past*

Ex: "I know I'm right," he said.

→ He said (that) he knew he was right.

2) *present continuous* → *past continuous*

Ex: "I'm reading," she said.

→ She said (that) she was reading.

3) present perfect ➔ past perfect

    Ex: "I've just eaten the cake," he said.

➔ He said (that) he had just eaten the cake.

4) will ➔ would

    Ex: "I'll probably come," Mary said.

➔ Mary said (that) she would probably come.

5) simple past ➔ past perfect

    Ex: "I wasn't there during the scandal," John said.

➔ John said (that) he hadn't been there during the scandal.

6) be going to ➔ was / were going to

    Ex: "I'm going to call on them," Alice said.

➔ Alice said (that) she was going to call on them.

7) must ➔ does not change

    Ex: "I must leave," Ann said.

➔ Alice said (that) she must leave.

NOTES

- *If we refer to something true in any situation, the tense of the verb does not change*
- *We change the reference to people, places and time, because the point of view changes*

VERBS THAT COULD BE CONFUSED

- Speak = the action of speaking
- Say = describes words (optionally followed by THAT)
  = cannot be followed by a pronoun ➔ in such situation we have to change it with **tell**
    Ex: She said to her brothers.
       but: She told me.
- Tell = offers information ➔ requires a direct object (optional followed by THAT)

NOTES:

1) we use TELL + INF. To express orders.
Ex: "Go there!" he told me. ➔ He told me to go there.

2) WHETHER ➔ we use it for questions including OR
Ex: "Are you coming with me or going with them?" he asked.
➔ He asked me whether I was going with him or with them.

3) questions in reported speech do not require inversion
Ex: "What are you doing?" he asked me.
   He asked me what I was doing.

4) if there is an introductive question before the question in the reported speech, then the tense in the reported question does not change

ENGLISH GRAMMAR PRACTICE

Ex: "Could you show me where the show hall is," he asked.

→ He asked me if I could to show him the show hall.

Reporting verbs

⇨ **Include a part of the meaning of what is reported**

ADVISE (IF I WERE YOU)	INVITE
AGREE	AFTER
APOLOGIZE	PROMISE
ASK	REFUSE
CONGRATULATE	REMIND
DECIDE	SUGGEST

UNIT 27: PRACTICE REPORTED SPEECH

1. *Rewrite the sentences in reported speech, beginning as shown:*

a) "I'm coming to you now," John told me.

   John told _____.

b) "We want a break, please!" the students said.

   The students said _____.

c) "Dan has just left!" Mary told me.

   Mary told me _____.

d) "The cat? It ate an hour ago," she said.

   She said _____.

e) "Luke didn't pass his exam," his mother told me.

   Luke's mother told _____.

f) "They will be back soon," Mary told us.

   Mary told _____.

g) "Mary is sleeping now," her sister told him.

   Her sister told _____.

h) "It will rain tomorrow," John said.

   John said _____.

i) "We'll be late! Hurry up!" I said.

   I said _____.

j) "You have lost it, damn it!" she said.

   She said _____.

English Grammar Practice

2. Rewrite the sentences in reported speech in direct speech:

a) She said that she had missed the train.
 "_____," she said.

b) We told them that the car was broken.
 "_____," we told them.

c) Mother asked them why they had missed the classes that day.
 "_____," mother asked them.

d) John told us that he had slept till late.
 "_____," John told us.

e) Sean and Andrew said that they wouldn't come with us.
 "_____," Sean and Andrew said.

f) The child asked its mother if she had bought him a toy.
 "_____," the child asked.

g) They called us and said that they had arrived on time.
 "_____," they said on the phone.

h) Sheila told me that she was going to leave soon.
 "_____," Sheila told me.

i) They said that they had written a note for me.
 "_____," they said.

j) You told me that you would be there on time.
 "_____," you told me.

English Grammar Practice

3. Correct the errors in the following sentences:

a) She said me that she would come next day.

b) They told us that they did their homework already.

c) Melanie said that she is ill.

d) Mother and father told us that they come back at three.

e) Lucy and Dan said that they were dancing all night the other day.

f) Betty and I told them that we wrote two letters to Aunt Alice so far.

g) He said that he is going to leave the town.

h) You told them that you led John to the airport.

i) The boy told his mother that his class is going to take a trip to Manchester.

j) We told to the teacher that we are just writing the essay.

4. Rewrite the sentences in reported speech:

a) "Go to the store, John," mother said.

b) "Come to us on Friday, Mary," we said.

c) "Let's have dinner, children," mother told us.

d) "Go back to your seat," the professor told the student.

e) "Don't ask silly questions," I told him.

f) "Leave that on the table and get out," he told me angrily.

g) "Stop saying that all the time," Mark told her.

h) "Take the bus from the corner of that street," I told them.

i) "Go to visit the castle," the man told the tourists.

j) "Don't ask so many questions," mother told the children.

5. Fill in the blanks with one of the verbs given in the right tenses:

tell, want, ask, apologise, advise, congratulate, agree, promise

a) She _____ me that I had to go there in the afternoon.

b) We _____ them not to take tickets to that show.

c) I _____ to have a black coffee and I said that

d) John _____ Ann because she had passed her exam.

e) William _____ to come with us.

f) John _____ the librarian to give him that book.

g) He _____ to bring them the tapes.

h) They _____ because they had made such a blunder.

i) We _____ with their idea.

j) She _____ to come earlier that day.

English Grammar Practice

6. Rewrite the sentences in reported speech using a verb in the list:

suggest, propose, refuse, agree, apologise, remind, invite, ask, offer, advise, congratulate

a) "I wouldn't go there if I were you," John told Ann.
b) "Let's go to the cinema tonight," I said.
c) "Shall I take your bag?" the boy asked.
d) "I'll give it to you, to be sure," Alice said.
e) "I won't do it," George said.
f) "Your idea is very good! We should apply it!" he said.
g) "Well done, Alice! You've taken your driving license," mother told Alice.
h) "I'm sorry I haven't come on time," Mel said.
i) "You have to go there, remember?" Stan told me.
j) "Why don't you join us for the party?" the boy said.
k) "Okay, we'll come to the festival," they said.
l) "Can you lend me your book for today?" his colleague asked him.

7. Rewrite the sentences in reported speech:

a) "Have you brought the tickets or not?" John asked me.
b) ""Will you come with us?" they asked her.
c) "Are you staying at the hotel this summer?" Peter asked Dan.
d) "Are you going to take that day off?" he asked me.
e) "Have you been to Cambridge this week?" Alice asked them.

English Grammar Practice

f) "Were you doing your work when I phoned you?" Paul asked me.

g) "Will you work with us tomorrow again?" Donna asked them.

h) "Have you spent a lot in town?" father asked Jill.

i) "Are you eating now?" mother asked Alan.

j) "Have they already got there?" my cousin asked me.

8. *Rewrite the questions in reported speech, as shown:*

a) "When did you come back?" I asked.

    I asked him _____.

b) "Why are you so late?" he asked her.

    He asked _____.

c) "What are you doing there?" he asked the boy.

    He asked _____.

d) "Where have you been?" she asked me.

    She asked _____.

e) "How much does it cost?" I asked the baker.

    I asked _____.

f) "How long have you been doing that?" the little girl asked her brother.

    The little girl _____.

g) "When are you coming back?" I asked Ann.

    I asked _____.

h) "Where does she live?" I asked him.

    I asked him _____.

i) "When does the shop close?"

    Do you know _____?

j) "What does this thing mean?"

    Could you tell me _____?

English Grammar Practice

SOLUTION OF THE EXERCISES

UNIT 2: PRACTICE PRESENT TENSE AND PRESENT CONTINUOUS TENSE

1. goes, lives, writes, answers, touches, misses, does, reads, studies, plays, enters

2. a) is, wakes up, goes, washes, gets dressed, goes, has, drinks, eats, washes, leaves, takes, must, leaves, delivers, comes, finishes, goes, arrives, has, reads, watches, has, takes, goes

3. a) Does he go to school every day? - No, he sometimes goes to the stadium.
b) I go to the theatre twice a month. Do you go to the theatre too? - Yes, I do, but I go only once a month.
c) Do they go to their aunt's house in the country every summer? – No, they don't, only Keith does.

4. a) Do you learn well?
b) Does John sleep in the afternoon?
c) Do they come to the sea every year?
d) Does she drive to office every morning?
e) Does your grandmother feel well usually?

English Grammar Practice

5. going, touching, dying, quarrelling, putting, asking, dropping, lying, studying, seeing, writing

6.
a) You are living with your friends these days.
b) They are coming with us to the cinema this afternoon.
c) Liz is reading in her room now.
d) They are driving to the sea this week.
e) We aren't learning for the exam today.
f) Is John going to the circus now?
g) Are Joshua and Ann eating their lunch at the moment?
h) Aren't you coming with them to the show?
i) Is he writing the letter right now?
j) We spend time with friends every Sunday

7. *(a)*
He gets up at nine o'clock every day but today he is getting up at seven. He usually drinks tea at breakfast but today he is having coffee. He dresses in a suit for work every morning but today it is Saturday and he dresses casual clothes. He is driving to the sea with Tom in his car now.

(b)
John is a history teacher. He spends a lot of time at school every day. Today he is spending five hours. He teaches the history of the world. He is teaching Ancient History today. He is upset because the children aren't paying attention in class now.

8.
- a) Do they sometimes come to you?
- b) Are you going with them to church today?
- c) Is it getting warmer every day?
- d) Are we driving to office this morning?
- e) Is he writing a novel these days?
- f) Is she knitting a pullover for her sister?
- g) Are you living with your parents this week?
- h) Is she sleeping at the house?
- i) Do they usually learn in the morning?
- j) Does he never do his homework?

9.
- a) He likes going to the swimming pool in the afternoon.
- b) She is tasting your cake now.
- c) The food tastes better now. You have put some spices, haven't you?
- d) Leonora needs a new bike. Hers is broken.
- e) We own a bigger house now.
- f) The book belongs to John. It's a present from Ann.
- g) I realise that I've made a mistake.
- h) She is thinking of her work at the moment.
- i) John thinks he is right and he is.
- j) I expect you succeed. I am expecting news from you after the exam.

10.
- a) John and Ann like the food today.
- b) I'm thinking of my holiday now.
- c) We go to school in the mornings.
- d) They are living with their friends this year.
- e) She swims quite well.
- f) It smells good in the kitchen. They've made a cake.
- g) The rose smells good. I love it.
- h) I see Alice across the street.
- i) They agree with you in this matter.
- j) I like to dress casually.

11.
- a) I am ready to go with you to school.
- b) They have a new job in the other town.
- c) Joshua is going to Glasgow next week.
- d) She has a new sports car.
- e) You are my best friend.
- f) They are leaving this afternoon.
- g) Robert is a good swimmer, indeed.
- h) They are not what we imagined. They are only freshmen.
- i) You don't have any right to come here and say that.
- j) She is not leaving now. She is staying some more time.

12.
- a) Ann <u>is going</u> to the circus this evening.
- b) They <u>listen</u> to the news every day.
- c) It <u>is raining</u>. I've taken my umbrella.
- d) Lucy and Dan <u>live</u> in a house near the sea.
- e) They <u>aren't going</u> to Paris next year.
- f) We <u>spend</u> a lot of time in the library. We <u>study</u>
- g) <u>am looking</u> for a book on this subject.
- h) Mary has a new job. She <u>works</u> in a hospital.
- i) The children <u>are being</u> naughty today. They <u>aren't listening</u> to anything they're told.
- j) You <u>write</u> nice letters.

English Grammar Practice

UNIT 3: PRACTICE PRESENT TENSE – 2

1.

a) You are in the classroom and you don't know what your colleagues are talking about. You ask a colleague nearby:

   2. Please, tell me what is about. Do you know?

b) You are in the street and you don't know the direction to the post-office. You ask a passerby:

   3. Could you tell me where the post-office is?

c) You are in a shop with a friend. You want to buy a dress but you can't make up your mind. You ask your friend:

   2. Can you tell me which fits me best?

d) You want to rent a flat but you don't know any. You ask a friend:

   1. I want to rent a flat. Do you know any?

e) You need a book from a friend to write an essay. You say:

   3. Could you lend me this book? I need it, please.

f) You are visiting a friend in hospital. You ask him:

   1. How do you feel? Is it better?

g) You meet an old friend in the street and find out he has a new job. You ask:

   2. Do you go on with your new job?

h) You want to visit a friend and you call him. You say:

   2. What do you think? May I come to you?

i) You need a new coat. You tell your mother:

   2. Can you buy me a new coat? I need one.

j) You want to invite a friend to the swimming pool. You say:

   3. I'm going to the swimming pool. Could you come too?

2.
   a) I'm going to the match tomorrow.
   b) He likes ice cream.
   c) They are coming to you every day now.
   d) She is feeling well today.
   e) I need a new book from the bookshop.
   f) She leaves for Miami every summer.
   g) We are going to the movie this evening.
   h) I'm hating this book!
   i) Alan wants to go with you.
   j) They realise they have made a mistake.

3.
   a) Noreen <u>is going</u> to the mountain with the Browns next week.
   b) What <u>does this action involve</u>?
   c) I <u>mean</u> it. I'm going to get very angry.
   d) Susan <u>is leaving</u> with them.
   e) George <u>always goes</u> to the movies on Saturday.
   f) He <u>is always breaking</u> something while washing dishes.
   g) Neil <u>comes</u> to visit you twice a year.
   h) I <u>prefer</u> tea.
   i) She <u>needs</u> a new bag.
   j) I <u>recognize</u> her now. She's Ann's niece.

English Grammar Practice

4.

a) Is Lucy coming to you this afternoon? Lucy?

b) Are you going to the castle?

c) Do you learn Spanish?

d) Is she here now? Here?

e) Are you painting the house this spring?

f) Do you watch TV?

g) Do they study geography at school?

h) May I smoke here?

i) Do they have a dog?

j) Is she buying a car?

5.

a) I'm not going to the museum this afternoon.

b) She doesn't live in a house near the school.

c) They don't come to us once a month.

d) Ann and George aren't going to the show this evening.

e) He isn't having lunch at the moment.

f) She isn't doing her homework in her room.

g) The boys don't drive to college every morning.

h) Ann and John don't watch TV in the evening.

i) We aren't building a new house this summer.

j) She isn't staying with her brother for the moment.

6.
- a) Laura lives with her family in the suburbs.
- b) They play in the park in the afternoons.
- c) We don't need any new clothes this season.
- d) They are seeing their friends in the disco this evening.
- e) She never does her homework on time.
- f) The children are going with their parents to the circus on Sunday.
- g) She and I are seeing each other these days.
- h) We don't ever misinform the committee.
- i) You don't rest enough and that is why you are so tired.
- j) I don't send him any letter. (not send)

7.

writing	living
seeing	quarrelling
dropping	eating
being	studying

English Grammar Practice

8.
- a) She isn't reading a novel now.
- b) Don't they live in the country?
- c) She is coming to school today.
- d) The boy doesn't do his homework every day.
- e) Is he riding his bike in the neighbourhood at the hour.
- f) We aren't giving them a phone call at the moment.
- g) I am leaving to the theatre now.
- h) He doesn't work in an office in the harbour now.
- i) They don't go skating every winter.
- j) Are you coming at six?

9.
- a) Joshua <u>usually</u> goes to school on the bus.
- b) They are going to the doctor <u>in the afternoon</u>.
- c) She is listening to the news <u>at the moment</u>.
- d) This boy <u>normally</u> lives with his grandparents.
- e) Susie is <u>always</u> coming late to school.
- f) George doesn't <u>ever</u> read a book.
- g) Lucia and Ann read a lot <u>normally</u>.
- h) I am very attentive in class <u>now</u>.
- i) She is buying a new car <u>at the moment</u>.
- j) We <u>usually</u> have four classes a day.

10.
   a) They usually drive to office in the morning.
   b) She never stays late in town.
   c) He is coming with us to the sea this summer.
   d) Josh doesn't want to go with them to the theatre this evening.
   e) We are looking for that book in the bookcase for the moment.
   f) She is always leaving her clothes all over the floor!
   g) Tom is thinking of breaking up with Mary because he's very upset.
   h) The child is hungry. It is eating everything.
   i) Mrs. Smith is cooking dinner because people are coming to dinner. She usually cooks very well.
   j) Mary is crying in her room because she's lost her favourite ribbon.

11.
a) Are you coming to me this evening? - 8. Yes, I am. I'm not working this afternoon after program.
b) What are you doing at the moment? - 10. I'm having lunch and then I'm going to bed. I'm very tired.
c) They are going on a trip next week. What are you saying? – 2. I'm in France next week and I don't know when I come back.
d) She is going to the doctor this afternoon, I hear. What's wrong? - 1. I don't know. People say she's run down at the moment.

e) Mary and Tom are coming to visit us this evening. Are you at home? - 7. I'm having a meeting at the office and I might be too late.

f) You are too busy, I'm afraid. – 3. Yes, I know. I have a lot of work to do and I have no spare time at all.

g) Are you thinking of going to the mountains this winter? - 4. I don't think so. I don't have vacation until in the summer.

h) Lucy says she's buying a new car and driving to Paris next month. - 6. She is having an important interview there.

i) Are you playing basketball this weekend? - 5. I'm going to Quebec this weekend.

j) They are going to town. Do you need anything? - 9. I'm going shopping myself later.

12.
- a) It is raining and you must take your umbrella.
- b) It is very cold. – Yes, indeed. And the wind is blowing too.
- c) It smells good in the house. – Yes, mother is cooking.
- d) They are going shopping in town this afternoon. They always go shopping in the afternoon.
- e) They are at the bakers. They are buying some bread and cakes for tea.
- f) We are going to buy tickets for the theatre. Are you coming with us?
- g) She likes to drink a black coffee in the morning. She is drinking coffee now.
- h) Ann is calling me. I am going to the show with her.

i) They ride their motorcycles every weekend.

j) You are thinking of going to them next week, aren't you?

UNIT 4: PROGRESSIVE TEST

1.
   a) John likes playing football with his friends in the schoolyard every Saturday. He is playing football with them this Saturday too.

   b) They are doing their homework now. They always do their homework at this hour.

   c) She never calls us. We usually call.

   d) I am leaving by bus to Barrie this afternoon.

   e) This car doesn't belong to me.

   f) They mean they aren't going with you.

   g) What are you doing this afternoon? I am reading for my essay.

   h) She is coming to me this evening. We are going to Susan's party.

   i) Briana writes interesting compositions. She is presenting one at school tomorrow.

   j) Janice and Jean are having lunch in town tomorrow.

2.

2. is looking; 1. leave; 1. expect; 1. agree; 2. is expecting; 2. are driving;
2. is going; 1. want; 1. usually feels run down; 1. thinks;

3.
- a) I am not feeling well and I don't know if I can manage today.
- b) They are leaving for a short trip in the mountains this weekend.
- c) Kate's friends are coming to visit her today. They usually visit her once a month.
- d) She is having her birthday party this Saturday and she is inviting all her friends.
- e) We usually help our mother with the spring cleaning.
- f) They travel with their friends every year. This year they are travelling to London.
- g) I recognize you now. You are Mary's niece, aren't you?
- h) What are they doing? They are playing chess in their room and they are happy.
- i) He appreciates your work. You usually do a good job.
- j) Hurry up! The train is leaving the station.

4.
- a) He keeps not paying attention to what I'm saying.
- b) The English class begins at nine.
- c) Lauren doesn't ever visit us in summer.
- d) She's leaving the town on Sunday, there's no doubt.
- e) The end of the school year is in June.
- g) What about going to the disco?
- h) Are you thinking of going to them?
- i) You are wearing too many clothes.
- j) Which book belongs to you?

5.
- a) John's daughter plays the violin very well. She is playing in this concert at school.
- b) Do they go to the sea this summer? They usually go to the sea in July.
- c) We are spending our winter holiday in Quebec this year, even though we prefer going to Florida.
- d) I enjoy spending time with them. That is why I am going with them to the country this weekend.
- e) Ann spends too much and therefore she has no money at the end of the month.
- f) They are running this evening in the park. They want to keep themselves in a good shape.
- g) What time you do get up on Sundays? - I usually get up at ten, but during the week I get up at seven.
- h) I am going swimming today and I am thinking of inviting her too.

i) I've arranged to go to Madrid. I am spending a few days there with friends.

j) What does this business involve? Do I travel a lot?

6.
  a) She is spending her summer vacation in London.
  b) We don't like chocolate cakes too much.
  c) Sue and Dan are driving to work this morning.
  d) He is going on foot to office today.
  e) He plays football well.
  f) I don't care if you go there.
  g) It's not important if it rains today.
  h) How much does this shirt cost, please?
  i) Mother is going to the shops.
  j) I'm not sure if I want to go there.

7.
  a) We don't work too much <u>currently</u>.
  b) Georgia isn't listening to music <u>today</u>.
  c) My brothers don't play football <u>every day</u>.
  d) I <u>don't always have lunch</u> at three.
  e) He <u>is always boasting</u>.
  f) I'm working <u>till</u> five o'clock today.
  g) He isn't coming <u>before</u> nine.
  h) You <u>often don't come</u> on time.
  i) She <u>never knits</u> pullovers.
  j) Mandy and Kate don't do their job on time <u>always</u>.

8.
- a) She doesn't listen to music every Sunday.
- b) We never go camping over the weekend.
- c) She isn't going to the cinema today.
- d) Melanie is cleaning the room this afternoon.
- e) Mandy invites friends at home every Sunday.
- f) You are always leaving your clothes on the floor!
- g) He keeps bothering me all the time.
- h) The cake tastes good.
- i) I'm smelling the flowers in this pot. They smell good.
- j) Paula is sleeping because she is very tired and tomorrow she is meeting someone.

UNIT 6: PRACTICE PAST TENSES - 1

1.
- a) John is a bank director now, but he was a clerk bank last year.
- b) They are teachers now, but last year, they were office-workers.
- c) She is an optician now, but three years ago, she was a nurse.
- d) We are librarians now, but last year, we were salesmen.
- e) I am a writer now, but two years ago, I was a journalist.
- f) You are an engineer now, but a few months ago, you were a mechanic.
- g) He is an actor now, but two months ago, he was a shop assistant.
- h) Mary is a housewife, but two weeks ago, she was a librarian.
- i) They are students now, but last year, they were workers on a shipyard.
- j) Noreen is an executive assistant now, but two years ago, she was a student.

English Grammar Practice

2.

a) They were at school at 9 am.

b) They were in the cinema at four pm.

c) They were in hospital at noon.

d) They were on the bus at 8 am.

e) They were at John's anniversary in the evening.

f) They were with friends at the theatre at nine pm.

g) They were at the baker's at two pm.

h) They were at the newsagent's at 6 am.

i) They were on the plane at four pm.

j) They were in their car at ten am.

3.
- a) Where were you on Thursday afternoon?
- b) Where was she last Monday?
- c) Where were they last month?
- d) Where was he last year?
- e) Where were you when I phoned you?
- f) Where was she when you came?
- g) Where were you when they looked for you?
- h) Where were Mary and John when you called on them?
- i) Where was I when you brought that book?
- j) Where were we when the house was broken in?

4.

danced	cried	walked	talked
lived	studied	arranged	answered
died	dyed	settled	asked

5. (b)

She woke up at seven o'clock in the morning and went to the bathroom. Then she prepared breakfast for the family and the sandwiches for school for her children. Then she drove her children to school. After leaving them at school, she went shopping. When she came back home, she cleaned the house and prepared lunch for her children and herself. Then she did the washing up. In the afternoon, she read a magazine or watch TV. She did the laundry and ironed clothes or helped her children with their homework. In the evening, she prepared dinner for the entire family because her husband came back from work. She went to bed at eleven o'clock.

6.
- a) What did you do yesterday? – I had an invitation to the cinema.
- b) What did you have for breakfast yesterday? – I had tea.
- c) What did you do in the test on Monday? I did well.
- d) You had a meeting yesterday. Did you forget?
- e) She didn't listen to the teacher in class yesterday.
- f) They did their best as usual.
- g) We had a boat two years ago. Did you sail a lot? - Yes, we did.
- h) Martin and John had fight in the yard an hour ago.
- i) I had a white sports car a few years ago.
- j) The child had bread and butter for his snack yesterday.

7.
- a) Where did they go last year?
- b) What time did he wake up yesterday?
- c) Where did he spend his vacation?
- d) Did Lucy come to you yesterday?
- e) Did you leave early for school last year?
- f) When did Joshua and Mary meet in the park yesterday?
- g) How long ago did you study French?
- h) Did they introduce her to you?
- i) Where did the boys play football last Sunday?
- j) Did they sell the house last month?

8.
a) When did you meet them? - 4) I met them in winter last year.
b) What did you do in summer? - 8) I went with friends to mountains.
c) Why didn't you do your homework? - 1) I didn't know the exercise.
d) What time did they go there? - 7) They went there in the morning the other day.
e) Did he come back from Paris last week? - 2) No, he didn't. He came back two weeks ago.

f) Why did they lose their temper? - 10) Because she did that stupid thing.
g) Did she succeed in her exams? - 3) Yes, she did.
h) Who did they send the book to? - 6) They sent it to their friends.

English Grammar Practice

i) What time did the show start last night? - 5) It started at eight pm.

j) Did you buy the newspaper in the morning? - 9) No, I'm sorry. I forgot. I know it is too late now.

9.
- a) While we were watching TV, someone knocked at the door.
- b) Our dog was barking in the yard.
- c) When I opened the door, I saw John, our neighbour, who was standing in front of the door.
- d) I listened to what he told me and I invited him to sit down.
- e) He sat down and told me about what happened to him.
- f) After he left, I cooked the dinner.
- g) They were watching TV, while I was cooking dinner.
- h) Then, I washed the dishes.
- i) While I was washing the dishes, the others were watching TV and they were laughing.
- j) I left the kitchen too, and watched TV with them afterwards.

10.
- a) He was reading while Mary was cleaning the bathroom.
- b) She was writing a letter when she was on vacation.
- c) I saw Alice just as she was getting into the office.
- d) The dog barked when the thief broke into the house.
- e) He told that story when we went together on the trip.
- f) I was listening to the tape when mother arrived.
- g) While Mary was cleaning the house, Elaine was dusting the furniture.
- h) Adrian saw them when they were walking in the park.
- i) Father was digging in the garden when it started to rain.
- j) Mrs. Smith was reading a report when her secretary entered the room.

11.

    a) The boy <u>was playing</u> football when his father <u>came</u> home.

    b) She <u>was listening</u> to the radio when I <u>got</u> into the room.

    c) While <u>was drawing</u>, the pencil-case <u>fell</u>.

    d) She <u>was driving</u> to the sea when a police officer <u>stopped</u> her.

    e) Wendy <u>was playing</u> the piano while Maria <u>was playing</u> the violin.

    f) When he <u>entered</u> the office, the secretary <u>was typing</u> a letter.

    g) While they <u>were swimming</u>, it <u>started</u> to rain.

    h) The children <u>were talking</u> when the teacher <u>came</u>.

    i) He <u>was teaching</u> the new lesson when Mary <u>knocked</u> on the door.

    j) Louise <u>was talking</u> over the telephone when her mother <u>came</u> back home.

12.

    a) She was driving <u>when</u> she saw the accident.

    b) He saw the girl <u>just as</u> she was getting into the room.

    c) She was writing a letter <u>the moment</u> the bell rang.

    d) I saw a few fellows in front of the theatre <u>when</u> I went to meet her.

    e) The woman was reading a good novel <u>when</u> the telephone rang.

f) She saw her two weeks <u>ago</u>.
g) Yesterday, I saw Alice <u>while</u> I was walking in the street.
h) They saw him <u>the other day</u>.
i) Sheila was leaving the house <u>when</u> I came back.
j) I didn't read that book <u>yesterday</u>.

UNIT 7: PRACTICE PAST TENSES - 2

1.
- a) John <u>lived</u> at the country last year.
- b) Sue and Ann came to us while we <u>were having</u> lunch.
- c) He <u>was driving</u> to the country when he <u>had</u> the accident.
- d) The riders <u>stopped</u> on the top of the hill when they <u>heard</u> that scream.
- e) The woman <u>was leaving</u> the shop when she <u>saw</u> the coat.
- f) They <u>built</u> a vacation house last year.
- g) We <u>were eating</u> when Aunt Mary <u>dropped by</u>.
- h) Lucy and Dan <u>were playing</u> cards while their brother <u>was watching</u> TV.
- i) When I <u>left</u> the house, it <u>was raining</u> hard and the wind <u>was blowing</u>.
- j) The class <u>had started</u> when he <u>came</u>.

2.

a) Did they leave the house and drive to work at ten o'clock yesterday?

b) Susan and David didn't come to us the other day.

c) They agreed with his idea at the meeting on Thursday.

d) She bought a new dress last week.

e) We didn't drive to work yesterday morning.

f) Joshua didn't spend a lot of money the other day.

g) Did they book tickets for Paris last week?

English Grammar Practice

h) Did she never leave the town last year?

i) We didn't go to the sea last summer.

j) Was she telling the truth during the investigation?

3.
- a) He went there while I was waiting for him.
- b) She saw the boy just as he was getting into the car.
- c) We met in London years ago.
- d) Last year, they opened a bookshop in our town.
- e) They met in front of the station at 9:15.
- f) How long ago did you meet him at the hank?
- g) She didn't pass her exams last month.
- h) They were riding their bikes at the time.
- i) I left the room when he entered.
- j) Susie came to us an hour ago.

4.

a) Did Alice come to you the other day? - 5) Oh, yes, she did. She stayed for half an hour.

b) When did you meet John in town? - 9) Last week I think.

c) Did they leave the country? – 1) Yes, they did, indeed. Last week.

d) When did you book the tickets for your vacation? - 10) Two weeks ago, maybe. I wanted badly to go there.

e) Did they like the play? What do you think? - 7) I think so. They laughed a lot during the show.

f) Did you solve that issue? - 2) No, I didn't. Hannah tried to help me, but I didn't solve it.

g) Where did you go when you left the classes yesterday? - 4) I met my aunt in town. She came from the country.

h) Why didn't you come to us on Friday? - 3) I wasn't in town that's all.

i) Did he write you a letter? I think he promised. - 6) Yes, he did, but I haven't received anything yet.

j) Laura returned from abroad. She finished the university. - 8) Did she? That is good for her. What did she do there?

5.
- a) Lucy came to us yesterday afternoon while we were watching the match on TV.
- b) She was ironing all the clothes while Fred was digging the garden.
- c) We didn't come to your party on Saturday because we had a problem with the child.
- d) Why didn't I write to you? Well, I don't know. Maybe I didn't have time.
- e) Louise felt bad yesterday and she lay in bed all day. She was still lying in bed when I came.
- f) They learnt French last year with Mrs. Denis. They liked her a lot. She taught well.
- g) The children played in the garden when their mother called them in.
- h) While I was writing my essay, the dog started to bark. He was barking to a man at the door.
- i) They didn't write to her a line at least and, therefore, she got very angry with them.
- j) He was always talking about race cars and that annoyed Mary.

English Grammar Practice

6.

laid	meant	ate
taught	received	travelled
spent	asked	sold

7.
a) We phoned to the police when we saw the accident.

b) Josephine was writing a letter to her friend in the country when John came and invited her to a show.

c) Alan and I met in the street the other day. I was going to my friend Jill at that moment.

d) Lucy and Dan were getting out of the car when we saw them and called their names.

e) Mr. Jones was dictating a letter to his assistant, Miss Smith, when the inspector came in.

f) When I was younger, I went to the Black Sea and met John on the beach.

g) Rita was playing chess with Richard when they heard the dog barking.

h) The two young people were talking when the waitress laid the plates on the table.

i) He was trying to solve a problem when Mary called him up and asked him about the result of the problem.

j) They were having a picnic when suddenly it started to rain.

English Grammar Practice

8.

a) What <u>were you doing</u> when he <u>knocked</u> at your door yesterday?

b) When <u>did he live</u> with you?

c) While he <u>was eating</u>, what <u>happened</u>?

d) She <u>was buying</u> a pair of socks in the shop when she <u>heard</u> the fire alarm and she <u>ran</u> out of the shop.

e) They <u>were answering</u> to the questions of the quiz when the bell <u>rang</u> and they <u>stopped</u>.

f) Louise and I <u>lived</u> with some friends that summer.

g) We <u>realised</u> that we had forgotten the bags in the car when we <u>were getting</u> inside.

h) It <u>was snowing</u> when the boys <u>went</u> skiing.

i) The cat <u>stole</u> the meat on the table when mother <u>turned</u> her back.

j) Their baby <u>was crying</u> when we <u>dropped</u> in.

9.

a) They <u>were lying</u> in bed when the bell <u>rang</u>. They worked a lot all that evening.

b) John heard he <u>had come</u> in town two days ago and went to see him.

c) She <u>had never believed</u> the story until she saw them and then she realised they <u>had said</u> the truth.

d) We remembered they <u>had come</u> to us before but we couldn't remember their faces.

e) She <u>was driving</u> down the road when she saw the kitten in the shadow of a tree.

f) They <u>had already left</u> when we came to their house.

g) The boy <u>had slept</u> all day yesterday and he didn't wake up when his parents came in the evening.

h) The teacher brought the tests they <u>had passed</u> the day before.

i) He <u>went</u> to the beach when he <u>was</u> young.

j) When he was a child, he <u>went</u> to his grandparents every summer.

10.

a) I <u>thought</u> I had the keys in my pocket but when I <u>got</u> to school I realised I <u>had forgotten</u> them at home.

b) They were sure they <u>had done</u> well in the test but when the teacher <u>brought</u> the tests they realised they <u>had made</u> a lot of mistakes.

c) She <u>met</u> them in the street yesterday and <u>told</u> them what she <u>had done</u> the day before.

d) We <u>were riding</u> our horses across the fields and we <u>were laughing</u> when suddenly we saw the clouds in the sky.

e) Mary <u>was leaving</u> the house when we <u>came</u> to visit her. She said she <u>had already got</u> an invitation to Mrs. Smith for tea and she had to leave.

f) The child <u>took</u> his bag and <u>left</u> as soon as he <u>had eaten</u>.

English Grammar Practice

g) He <u>had been digging</u> in the garden all day long and he was very tired when we <u>came</u>.

h) John and Ann remembered they <u>had met</u> him somewhere before.

i) Alice and Dan were sure they <u>had won</u> in the lottery and they had.

j) When he <u>came,</u> he asked me what I <u>had been doing</u> all afternoon. I answered that I <u>had been writing</u> letters.

11.

a) We were going to see the film last evening when our car broke in the middle of the road.

b) She realised she had forgotten to post the letter and she had to go back to the post-office.

c) The old man was crossing the street to go to the chemist's when the car came down the road and hit him.

d) She had been lying in bed all afternoon when I phoned her to see what she was doing.

e) The two boys had been playing football for two hours when the rain came down fast.

f) I had never seen her before but I thought that her face looked familiar to me.

g) My sister and I had been playing cards since noon, when mother came and told us to do our homework.

h) We went to Mary's house as soon as we had finished our homework.

i) By the time she got there, everyone had left.

j) They hadn't eaten anything until their mother came home from work that day.

12.
  a) She would / used to go to the sea every summer when she was very young.
  b) He would / used to eat anything when he was nervous.
  c) I used to hate schooldays when I was in the fifth form.
  d) They would / used to come to school late every day when they were in school.
  e) We wouldn't / didn't use to visit her too often because we didn't use to like her at all.
  f) She would always do such a thing in those days. / She always used to do such a thing in those days.
  g) Alex and Tom used to love the same girl last year.
  h) I would / used to go skiing every winter in my youth.
  i) You used to like this kind of food very much, indeed, when you were a child.
  j) He would / used to spend one month a year in his friends' house in the mountains.

English Grammar Practice

13.

a) She couldn't get into the house because her had forgotten her in the bag on the kitchen table at home.
b) She was a real bother for us because she always forgot everything.
c) No sooner had they got into the house than Mary came.
d) She had never cooked such a good meal before nor had I ever eaten one.
e) She had just entered the house when the telephone rang.
f) Scarcely had the dog got up when the boy put a bone onto his plate.
g) I'd never heard such a stupid thing like the one he told me.
h) The baby had already fallen when I tried to catch it.
i) By the time we got there to see him, he had already left.
j) Hardly had I entered the house when I had to leave again.

14.

a) No sooner <u>had I got</u> into the house than the phone <u>rang</u>.

b) They <u>reached</u> the airport in the end but the plane <u>had already left</u>.

c) That was the first coffee the woman <u>had drunk</u> that day.

d) It was the most embarrassing situation I <u>had ever seen</u>.

e) She <u>was driving</u> to the town when she realised she <u>had forgotten</u> to fill the tank.

f) We <u>had been reading</u> all evening when he <u>got</u> into the house.

g) When the sun <u>rose</u> <u>had been walking</u> on the beach for half an hour already.

h) By the time he <u>got</u> back home, the police <u>had left</u>.

i) Helen <u>had slept</u> by the time we <u>got</u> there.

j) They <u>sent</u> us a reply to our letter as soon as they <u>had received</u> it.

UNIT 8: CONSOLIDATION PAST TENSE

1.
   a) Mark <u>came</u> to her the moment she <u>was leaving</u> the office to go home.
   b) She <u>would go</u> to the Porters every summer when she <u>was</u> in the 5th form.
   c) Linda and Diane <u>were leaving</u> the cinema hall when we <u>saw</u> them.
   d) Nathan and I <u>had come</u> here by the time he <u>moved</u> into the school.
   e) I <u>didn't notice</u> anything but he <u>told</u> me what <u>had happened</u> before my arrival.
   f) Everyone <u>was crying</u> and <u>was shouting</u> and no one <u>kept</u> cool in the room.
   g) We <u>had never seen</u> such an interesting play before and therefore we <u>recommended</u> it to our friends.
   h) The girls <u>were talking</u> while the teacher <u>was explaining</u> the lesson and, therefore, he <u>got</u> very upset.
   i) He <u>used to like</u> swimming in the lake in his childhood.
   j) Lucian <u>didn't use</u> to own a car that year.

2.
- a) She had never visited them before so they hadn't met her until then.
- b) We drove to the country that morning and we met the Browns in an inn near Plymouth.
- c) She booked tickets for Edinburgh that day. I saw her in the travel agent's when she was paying the tickets. She greeted me and we talked for a while.
- d) The accounting office had completed the work until the economic inspectors came.
- e) She didn't use to go with them those days because she didn't like their company.
- f) Sue Ellen came home in the afternoon. She noticed at once her house had been broken into.
- g) The children had been playing cards all the afternoon when their mother came home from work.
- h) There were more people in the shop. Some people were buying some bread and cakes, others were looking around for some food and the others were expecting the new products to be exhibited.
- i) George and Alan had an appointment with their doctor that day and they met in order to go together.
- j) Last week, they visited the Smiths and had fun together. They made acquaintance long time ago and they spent time together now and then.

English Grammar Practice

3.
- a) We had never met him before and we were amazed to see that he was such a spoiled child.
- b) The director used to have a nice office with some new furniture and interesting decorations.
- c) They weren't sleeping when I got into their room and I minded that.
- d) You didn't come with us in the park last Sunday. What happened?
- e) The dog liked such a food and, therefore, I would give it to him at least every three days.
- f) Had you seen him before that night? – I hadn't, but I liked him at once.
- g) When I came home, the cat had been sleeping since morning.
- h) The child had been doing his homework since he came home.
- i) She had never seen such a beautiful flower before.
- j) The climbers had arrived at the cottage by noon.

4.
- a) They met that morning to go on a trip in the mountains. They were there before and they really liked the place.
- b) They left early to catch the first bus. They took rucksacks and torches with them.
- c) They reached the end of their trip by bus after they had been travelling for two hours.
- d) They started the climb and after two hours they reached a nice cottage in a sunny valley.
- e) They left the cottage after they ate and drank a little water.
- f) They had been climbing for three hours when they got onto the peak.
- g) They rested for a while before starting to walk again.
- h) They had been walking for more than four hours when they got back to the bus station.
- i) They took the bus after they had been waiting for more than half an hour.
- j) They had arrived in town by ten o'clock at night.

English Grammar Practice

5.
- a) No sooner <u>had they received</u> the telegram than they <u>booked</u> the tickets for the plane.
- b) They <u>had been working</u> for five hours when the telephone <u>rang</u> and <u>interrupted</u> them.
- c) They <u>hadn't seen</u> their aunt until they <u>came</u> back in town.
- d) She <u>knitted</u> a pullover last year.
- e) They <u>bought</u> new furniture for their bedroom after they <u>moved</u> into a new flat.
- f) Their friends <u>had already left</u> the hotel when they <u>arrived</u> at their hotel.
- g) We <u>had graduated</u> high school by the time he <u>became</u> a freshman.
- h) Stan <u>was driving</u> to the country when he <u>had</u> an accident.
- i) They <u>hadn't bought</u> the dresses they <u>wanted</u> until they <u>received</u> their pay cheque.
- j) They <u>had already left</u> when the teacher <u>came</u> with the results of the test.

6.
- a) When his sister came to ask for him he had already left.
- b) He fell in love: she was the most beautiful girl he has ever seen.
- c) As soon as they settled the tents, they made the campfire at once.
- d) Scarcely had she woken up than she started working.
- e) Sheila and Joan would go to their grandparents every holiday.
- f) I had packed all the things by the time they came to pick me up.
- g) As soon as the car crashed, the police came.
- h) Once the lecture ended, the students left the university.
- i) Hardly had he finished decorating his cottage in the mountains than his cousin asked him to let him go there for a week.
- j) It was the fourth glass of juice she had drunk.

7.
- a) He had left the schoolyard <u>when</u> I came.
- b) My brother and I would go to the camp <u>every holiday</u>.
- c) We realised that Joshua and Ann had met <u>before</u>. They were good friends.
- d) Lillian remembered she had forgotten the window open <u>when</u> she left the house.
- e) We had <u>already</u> eaten by the time mother woke up.
- f) The teacher had <u>just</u> entered the classroom <u>when</u> the fire alarm went off.
- g) You had been reading <u>since</u> noon when we came, hadn't you?
- h) I had seen the play <u>before</u> and therefore, I told them to go too.
- i) He was tired because he had been reading the reports <u>all night</u>.
- j) She recognized him <u>at once</u>. He was the man who smiled to her in the train.

8.
- a) No sooner **had he put** the receiver in the hook than the phone **rang** again.
- b) They **put** their books into their bags as soon as the class **had ended**.
- c) The child **had bought** the books by the time I **came** home.
- d) No one **believed** when he **told** us what **had happened** the day before.
- e) The sun **had already set** down when the group **got** into the glade.
- f) We **were getting** into the cinema hall when he **saw** us. We **entered** together and **sat** down. When the lights **went** out the film **started**.
- g) The vase with flowers **fell** off the table on the floor when the cat **hit** it.
- h) The children **entered** the house as soon as the wind **had started** to blow and it **had started** to rain.
- i) They **used to** like going to the beach on sunny days.
- j) No one **understood** what he **was saying** because the noise was overwhelming.

English Grammar Practice

UNIT 10: PRACTICE PRESENT PERFECT – 1

1.
- a) I'm from England but I live in Paris now. I have been living here since 1996.
- b) I'm a broker. I work for an insurance company in Paris. I have been working there for five years.
- c) I'm married to Tom. We had been married since 1992.
- d) Tom is a teacher. He has been teaching for five years already.
- e) We have been living in the same house for two years.
- f) We have bought our car since 1992.
- g) We are going on vacation in Greece this year. We have been planning this vacation for two months.
- h) We have booked the tickets since two weeks now.
- i) Tom has invited his sister to go with us since last month.
- j) She has been making plans for the trip ever since.

English Grammar Practice

2.

How long has she been living in Paris?

How long has she been working for an insurance company in Paris?

Since when have they been married?

How long have they been living in the same house?

Since when have they bought their car?

How long have they been planning the vacation?

Since when have they booked the tickets? Etc.

3.
- a) Have you ever eaten exotic food?
- b) He's left with Tom since noon.
- c) I've never been here before.
- d) She's just done her homework and already gone out.
- e) I've walked with Mary in the park for one hour.
- f) How long has she written on this novel?
- g) We've been working in the same place for five years.
- h) She's been waiting for me for half an hour.
- i) They've read in their room for three hours.
- j) She's never met Dan before.

English Grammar Practice

4.
- a) I've already washed my clothes.
- b) He's just listened to the news.
- c) She's ironed the tablecloth before.
- d) He's just left.
- e) They've played so far.
- f) She's already bought the newspaper.
- g) She's written letters before.
- h) They've sung up to now.
- i) They've just had breakfast.
- j) He's seen his friends off to the bus station before.

5.
- a) They <u>haven't learnt</u> for the exam yet.
- b) The child <u>read</u> the novel an hour ago.
- c) She <u>has written</u> the letters so far.
- d) They <u>have done</u> their homework for an hour.
- e) I <u>visited</u> them before lunch.
- f) We <u>have heard</u> the news before.
- g) They <u>have left</u> since noon and they <u>haven't come back</u> yet.
- h) They <u>went</u> to walk in the woods yesterday.
- i) Lucy <u>drove</u> to the country the other day.
- j) She <u>has cooked</u> dinner up to now.

6.

    a) It is the first time she has come here in her life.

    b) This evening, the boy hasn't eaten anything yet but he usually eats quite a lot in the evening.

    c) I've come to this school since we moved into this neighbourhood.

    d) They learn well at school and do all their homework. Today they have worked since four o'clock.

    e) I didn't have a car last year. I bought my car in April.

    f) I don't usually drink tea in the morning, but yesterday I drank some.

    g) Last year, we drove to the sea and the trip took five hours. Today, we have been driving to the sea for two hours and we have already passed by your town.

    h) They call us up at three or four everyday, but today they haven't called so far and it's about six in the evening.

    i) They are the most intelligent students I have ever had.

    j) I had an old car last year and it didn't run very well. I bought a new one in March and it has run just fine ever since.

7.

   a) *Crossing Jordan* is tonight on TV. Have you ever seen it? – No, not yet. Is it good?

   b) When did you go there last time? – I don't know for sure, but I think I haven't been there for two years.

   c) Have you seen him recently? – No, I haven't seen him for a few days, I suppose.

   d) May I see Ellen? Is she at home? – No, I'm afraid you've missed her. She left a few moments ago.

   e) Where were you at noon yesterday? – At school, I think. Why? – I wanted to talk to you and I didn't find you anywhere.

   f) How long have you been studying French? – For five years. Why? – You speak very well.

   g) Have you seen Mary lately? – No, I haven't. Why? – I hear she is in hospital. She has broken her leg.

   h) Where was your brother the other day? – I don't know for sure, but I suppose he played football with his pals.

   i) Have you read anything interesting lately? – Actually, I have. I have read Ludlum's new book.

   j) Have you read my offer? – Yes, but I don't think it fits our interests.

8.
- a) John has left already so you can't see him.
- b) I haven't met him yet so I don't know too much about him.
- c) Alice and Dan made acquaintance in March last year and they have been friends ever since.
- d) Carla and I left early yesterday morning, but we got late to school.
- e) Up to now I haven't done too much in the house. I have had no time.
- f) She has already gone to bed but I'll wake her up if you want.
- g) Denis and I met last night in town and went together to a restaurant.
- h) We have missed the plane, I'm afraid. It has already taken off.
- i) I have just heard some interesting news. Mary has won two competitions already.
- j) We haven't seen this movie before so we'll enjoy it.

UNIT 11: PRACTICE PRESENT PERFECT – 2

1.
- a) I have been writing translation exercises all morning.
- b) He has been reading all evening. I think he is going to bed soon.
- c) The girl is talking on the phone. I think she has been talking for twenty minutes now.
- d) Joshua has been sleeping all afternoon.
- e) He went to bed a few moments ago.
- f) They are coming to us this evening. – They have been coming to you all week.
- g) Do you see John there? – Yes, I think he is waiting for someone. He has been staying there for twenty minutes. I have been watching him all this time.
- h) What are you doing? – I am listening to a concert on the radio. I have been listening to it for an hour.
- i) The boy has been writing letters since two o'clock.
- j) What is Mary doing? – She is writing her reports. She has been writing for two hours.

English Grammar Practice

2.

a) Mel left by car for Berlin at noon. He has been driving since noon. He hasn't arrived yet.

b) What are you listening to? – I'm listening to an English language tape. I have been listening to it since breakfast. I have listened to six lessons already.

c) David is playing football. He has been playing for two hours. He played yesterday too.

d) She has just come inside. She has walked for a while. She usually walks in the afternoon.

e) The girls are having a chat. They have been talking for two hours. They meet in the afternoons and talk for hours.

f) They went to the cinema an hour ago. They are in the cinema hall now. The film has started. It has been running for half an hour.

g) I went to Maria's at three o'clock. We have been talking for an hour and waiting for Anna to come too. She hasn't come yet.

h) The boys meet once a week to play cards. They started playing at five this afternoon. They are playing now. They have been playing for two hours.

i) Alan is sleeping now. He went to bed half an hour ago. He has been sleeping for half an hour.

English Grammar Practice

    j) Mother is washing dishes. We have just had dinner. We are watching TV. We have been watching TV for a quarter of an hour.

3.

a) They have been living in the neighbourhood for two years.

b) I have walked since one o'clock.

c) He has been learning English for five years.

d) Mary has been writing this novel for two years.

e) We have worked here since 1992.

f) She has been reading since two o'clock.

g) It has been raining in the area for two weeks.

h) He has been sleeping since three o'clock.

i) They have been waiting for their guests for an hour.

j) She has been washing clothes for two hours.

4.

    a) How long ago did you move there?

    b) Josh hasn't come yet, I'm afraid.

    c) I am writing her address right now so have a seat for a minute.

    d) When did he come to you last night?

    e) I usually write to him quite often.

    f) She has been doing her homework all afternoon and she hasn't finished yet.

    g) Dan came to you last night.

English Grammar Practice

    h) I have eaten a cake so far so I'll have another one.

    i) We lost our books yesterday so we can't do our homework.

    j) Lydia has just left so you can't talk to her.

5.

    a) He <u>has gone</u> out of the room angrily because he <u>has had</u> a fight with his brother.

    b) John <u>broke</u> his sister's toy the other day.

    c) They <u>left</u> on a trip by car yesterday morning and they <u>have visited</u> two cities so far.

    d) Our children <u>play</u> with our neighbour's kids every day. They <u>played</u> yesterday too. They <u>have just come</u> to play with them. They are out in the yard now.

    e) She <u>started</u> playing the violin an hour ago. She <u>has already played</u> too much, don't you think?

    f) Where is Mary? – She <u>went</u> out with her friends an hour ago. She <u>has been walking</u> for an hour.

    g) I'm sorry I'm late. My watch <u>has stopped</u>. I <u>forgot</u> to wind it up last night.

    h) I <u>have finished</u> writing my reports for school, mother. May I go out? I <u>am going</u> with George to a film.

    i) They <u>have been driving</u> since ten o'clock in the morning. They <u>have already passed</u> by Brampton.

English Grammar Practice

j) I can't do my homework, mother. I <u>have understood</u> nothing in class today.

6.

a) John <u>has slammed</u> the door behind him. He <u>has just had</u> a row with Ann and he is furious.

b) We <u>went</u> to the sea last summer and this summer we <u>have gone</u> to the mountains.

c) The student <u>has just</u> put his work on the teacher's desk and he <u>has left</u> the classroom.

d) I <u>have just finished</u> my letter to Mary. I <u>wrote</u> ten pages.

e) I hear the dog barking. I think someone <u>has got</u> into our garden.

f) When I <u>came</u> home, I <u>saw</u> that there was a message on the answering machine. Someone <u>had called</u> and <u>left</u> a message.

g) Finally, I have a little peace. Our neighbour's guests <u>have left</u> and the music <u>has stopped</u>.

h) When I <u>got</u> to the bus stop, people <u>had been waiting</u> for half an hour and the bus <u>hadn't come</u> yet.

i) Turn the tape, please, it <u>has ended</u>.

j) Yesterday, it <u>had been snowing</u> since morning and it <u>hadn't stopped</u> all day.

7.

a) They have been coming to us since we met them.

b) We've been fixing the car since one o'clock.

c) He has been giving his speech since two o'clock.

d) They've been studying German since they came to this school.

e) She has been playing the piano since three o'clock.

f) They have been living in this town for ten years.

g) Mother has been cooking lunch for two hours.

h) He has been driving to Cambridge since dawn.

i) Oh, bother! He has been reading the newspaper since breakfast!

j) The students have been writing the test for an hour.

8.

a) Do you know what they did the other day? - 5) I'm not very sure, but I think they went to the swimming pool.

b) Have you solved the problem? - 7) Not yet, but I'm still trying.

c) What was he doing when you came to his place on Monday? - 10) I think he was having a shower.

d) Did you see her on Sunday? – 1) Yes, I did. She had been playing tapes when I came to her.

e) How long have you been studying German? - 8) For ten years and I think I manage quite well.

f) Did you notice anything strange when you got there? - 9) Yes, I think they were fighting.

English Grammar Practice

g) Have they written to you? - 4) Yes, I received two letters so far.

h) They have left, haven't they? - 2) Yes, they have. I saw them a few minutes ago.

i) She did it, didn't she? - 6) Oh, yes! She left him.

j) Have you bought a car? - 3) Not yet, but I'm still looking for one.

9.

a) She's just gone to the shops.

b) He's attended our university for two months.

c) John has been studying German since September.

d) She hasn't done her homework yet so she can't go out.

e) Mother has just left the house and gone to Aunt Alice.

f) Mother I've finished five cakes so far.

g) I haven't met him for a long time.

h) John hasn't gone to the sea before.

i) I've lost my wallet, I'm afraid.

j) He doesn't have the same mind with you anymore.

10.

a) It's ages since I've seen him.

b) He hasn't been there for a long time.

c) He has been to two concerts so far.

d) She has read twenty pages already.

e) They have forgotten their books.

f) He had been eating since 9 when I came.

g) I have lived here since 1989.

h) We have left to Paris by train since ten.

English Grammar Practice

i) She has been knitting this pullover since March.

j) She had been wearing her bag since June.

English Grammar Practice

UNIT 12: PROGRESS TEST

1.

a) I have been playing the violin since I was five.

b) She has been listening to that radio concert since she came back from school.

c) We have been writing letters for an hour.

d) She had finished writing her homework by the time I came.

e) Scarcely had we come back home than the telephone rang.

f) Her behaviour has changed and now she is quite rude.

g) They had written to us by March.

h) We have stopped listening to music so often.

i) Who does this car belong to?

j) Mary had been drawing since morning when I got there .

English Grammar Practice

2.

a) Alice has left the office and she has just got into the car, he pointed out.

b) Daniel and Alex have been training in the gym all day long. They haven't finished.

c) Dorian and I have been waiting for Mary since one o'clock. I think we should leave.

d) The child has been sleeping all afternoon and hasn't woken up yet.

e) Marilee and Josh have been married for thirty years.

f) Lucille had been working on that project for four hours when we came.

g) I had been presenting the commercial twenty minutes when the fire alarm got off.

h) So far, we haven't visited the Art Museum, but this month we have visited the History Museum twice.

i) Dan has lost his wallet and he is broke. Can you lend him some money?

j) He came last night and asked me the history book for a few days.

3.

    a) Where have you been? <u>I've been waiting</u> here for two hours.

    b) <u>Have you learnt</u> your lessons for tomorrow? – Yes, I have.

    c) He <u>has been speaking</u> to Mary on the phone since eight and he hasn't finished yet.

    d) He <u>has been working</u> in his room since eight and he will continue to do so until four.

    e) How long <u>have you lived</u> in this town? <u>I've lived</u> here since 1987 and I will continue to do so.

    f) The TV is on. He is in front of the TV. <u>He's been watching</u> TV for a long time.

    g) George is putting his pen down on the desk. <u>He's just finished</u> his homework.

    h) The teacher is speaking to his students. <u>He's been speaking</u> for half an hour.

    i) <u>They've swum</u> in the sea for an hour. <u>They've just left</u>.

    j) Father <u>has left</u> the flat.

4.

1. Where have you been?

　　b) I've been looking for you everywhere!

2. I'm sorry I'm late. Have you been waiting for long?

　　a) I've waited for fifteen minutes!

3. Has he already come?

　　a) Yes, he has. He's been watching TV since he came.

4. I'm here now. What have you done so far?

　　a) I've eaten my lunch. Now, I'm watching a film.

5. She's left since noon. What do you think she's doing?

　　a) She's driving. She's been driving for a long time.

6. Where's Jack?

　　a) He's in the bathroom. He's having a bath. He's been having a bath for ten minutes already.

7. Has the plane landed already? Where's Ann?

　　b) Yes, it has. Ann's clearing customs. She's been clearing customs for five minutes.

8. What's happened?

　　b) The car has stopped. We've arrived at Aunt Jane's place.

9. Have you finished the book already?

　　b) No, I haven't. I'm still reading it. I've been reading for the last three hours.

10. Where's my sweater?

　　a) Doris has taken it. She's been wearing it for three days.

5.
- a) They have been married for twenty years.
- b) She has been listening to the news for ten minutes.
- c) The baby has been crying for five minutes.
- d) They have been taking driving lessons for two weeks.
- e) They have been working in this factory for five years.
- f) She has been reading the reports for an hour.
- g) She has been staying with her cousin for two days.
- h) They have been driving from Bucharest to Constantza for an hour.
- i) She's been watering the flowers in the garden for half an hour.
- j) They have been in the park for half an hour.

6.
1. What exactly does he work?
2. Why is he in bed? He is in bed because he has caught flu.
3. Do you see that car? It's red.
4. It's getting dark. What are you doing now?
5. She's sleeping. She has been sleeping for five hours.
6. The sun has risen right now. It's in the sky.
7. They haven't learnt enough and they cannot pass the exam.
8. Who does this car belong to?
9. She hasn't come so far. We're still waiting for her.
10) What's he doing? He's writing. He has been writing for ten minutes.

7.
a) She is been saying stupid things.
b) He does not like to go out.
c) She is looking at him insistently.
d) Never mind his opinion, do it!
e) What is happening?
f) I'm quite run down.
g) How much does this road measure?
h) What do you think about having lunch in town today?
i) I am too busy with work to think of taking a day off.
j) He's going sailing for a few hours.

English Grammar Practice

8.
   a) She is teaching a new lesson.
   b) They keep asking questions!
   c) Is he here already?
   d) They aren't here anymore so you can't speak to them.
   e) The bus has left the bus station.
   f) They have lost their bags.
   g) She has been singing for an hour.
   h) George has just got out.
   i) Mary has gone into town.
   j) The departure of the bus is at one o'clock.

9.
   a) John has come in town already.
   b) He has known them since ages.
   c) They are studying for that test at the hour.
   d) She is always doing that.
   e) She has come here before.
   f) They are looking for the cat right now.
   g) They want to make a trip to Budapest.
   h) He is looking for his dog. He's been looking for it for five hours.
   i) It's a mess! We've just been moving furniture around.
   j) He likes that movie a lot.

10.
- a) They hadn't eaten anything until I came home.
- b) We normally write to them once a month.
- c) They usually get up early because they don't like to be late.
- d) He had no sooner got off the bike than the car hit him.
- e) They met in that resort last year.
- f) So far she's read every new book in that bookshop.
- g) They haven't seen each other too much lately.
- h) She left the house at nine a.m.
- i) We've just posted the letters for our friends.
- j) They've bought their new house recently.

UNIT 14: PRACTICE FUTURE - 1

1.
- a) Have you ironed the clothes, Jane? – Oh, no, I have forgotten. I will iron them now.
- b) Have you done your report, John? – No, I will do it now.
- c) Have you watered the flowers, Alice? – Oh, I've forgotten! I will water them now.
- d) Have you brought some bread? – No, I haven't had time. I will buy some now.
- e) Have you woken John up? – No, not yet, I will wake him up now.
- f) What else can we do now? – I know, we will go to a movie.
- g) I'm really tired and I can't wait for the bus again! I will take a cab.
- h) I have finished my work for today. What can I do now? I know, I will watch TV.
- i) Have you bought the tickets for the film, dear? – No, I will buy two tickets right now.
- j) I'm hungry. I don't know what to eat. – Hmm! I will eat some sandwiches.

English Grammar Practice

2.
- a) They are going to leave on a trip next week.
- b) She is going to come to us on Thursday.
- c) They are going to have a meeting on Monday.
- d) I am going to cook a good meal on Sunday.
- e) You are going to study English this semester, as I can see.
- f) He is going to take a dog, I hear.
- g) I'm afraid they are going to move into another town.
- h) She is going to get married next year.
- i) John is going to leave the country this summer.
- j) I am going to attend the university this year.

3.
- a) Don't do that! You will stick yourself.
- b) Come with us! We are taking a trip to the mountains next week.
- c) She will come on time, you will see.
- d) Look out! You will fall!
- e) It's ringing at the door. It will be John, I think.
- f) Oh, you have done it! What are they going to say?
- g) They sky is quite black. It is going to rain.
- h) Our team will win the match.
- i) My throat is sour. I am going to be sick.
- j) She has bought a car. She is going to take driving lessons.

4.
   a) They are going to meet at noon tomorrow.
   b) I think it's going to rain in a few minutes.
   c) She visits friends every weekend.
   d) It will probably rain tomorrow.
   e) I'll fall! Help me!
   f) Who will win the next match?
   g) Perhaps I'll come to you tomorrow.
   h) They will come next week, you'll see.
   i) What time is she coming tomorrow?
   j) I will probably call on you.

5.
a) Don't do that! - 1) You'll hurt yourself!
b) You can't go out! - 2) It's going to rain.
c) Why don't you buy a new coat? - 1) You will look smarter.
d) Why do you want to sell your house? - 2) I'm going to move to London next month.
e) Have you listened to the radio? What's the weather forecast for tomorrow? - 1) It will snow tomorrow.
f) Her mother is bringing her a cat tomorrow. - 2) How is she going to call it?
g) I've decided to buy a car. - 2) When are you going to buy it?
h) She doesn't know what to cook tonight. 1) I think she'll cook some spaghetti.
i) I predict a score 2 – 4. - 1) I think it will be 1 – 2.

j) What about meeting at the cinema at three o'clock tomorrow afternoon? –1) I'll be there.

6.
- a) She isn't going to come tomorrow evening.
- b) I won't be here at noon.
- c) Will It snow tomorrow?
- d) Is Sheila going to go to the sea next summer?
- e) Will our team win?
- f) We aren't going to leave at noon.
- g) I'm not going to move out next week.
- h) They will win, I'm sure.
- i) Will they come back soon?
- j) Perhaps he won't come.

7.
- a) She <u>will come</u>, <u>you'll see</u>.
- b) Let's go! The plane <u>is going to take off</u> soon.
- c) Go to that show! You <u>will enjoy it</u>.
- d) He has bought a car because <u>he is going to take</u> driving lessons.
- e) I haven't found my geography book. – <u>I will lend</u>.
- f) Our class <u>is going to take</u> a trip to Spain.
- g) When <u>are you going to be</u> home?
- h) John doesn't think <u>he will be</u> back at five.
- i) Why is he going out now? – He <u>is going to buy</u> a newspaper.
- j) I've missed the train. – What <u>will you do</u> now?

8.

a) Can you come to my party tomorrow evening? - 2. Sorry, I'm going to the mountains.

b) What have you planned for tomorrow? - 2. I'm going to play volleyball with my friends.

c) What do you think the weather forecast for tomorrow is? - 1. I think it will rain tomorrow.

d) Answer the phone, please. Who do you think it is? - 1. It will be Mary. She must call me.

e) What do you say about meeting me at the café at seven tomorrow evening? - 1. I'll be there.

f) Mary is going to college next year. - 2. Really? What specialization is she going to take?

g) It would be nice to meet all of us on Sunday next week. - 2. What are you going to do then?

h) I've seen the new film in town. You should go too. - 1. You will like it.

i) There is a match between our team and theirs tomorrow. - 1. What will the score be?

9.
- a) They are leaving / are going to leave tomorrow morning. They have already bought the tickets.
- b) Sheila has finished lunch and she is thinking what to do. She decides that she will read a book.
- c) What are they doing / are they going to do on Saturday? – They are going / are going to go to the cinema.
- d) When do you think you will come to me? – I don't know for sure. Perhaps I will come on Sunday afternoon.
- e) What's the weather like tomorrow night? – I hear it will snow.
- f) What are they doing / are they going to do next week? – They are visiting / are going to visit their aunt.
- g) Has he written to her so far? – No, but he will probably write to her tomorrow.
- h) Your sister is going / is going to go to the disco on Friday evening. Are you going to accompany / are you accompanying her?
- i) Has he already left? – No, he is flying / is going to fly to Paris next week.
- j) Have they already come back from their vacation? – No, but they will probably come back next week.

English Grammar Practice

10.

a) She thinks our class will win in the competition.

b) They are going to go to a show tomorrow.

c) She will call them up now.

d) I will go there too.

e) They are going to move out.

f) John is having a party on Friday.

g) They are going to come back next weekend.

h) Where are you going for the holiday?

i) Okay! I will be outside the cinema at four.

j) They aren't going to change schools after all.

UNIT 15: PRACTICE FUTURE - 2

1.
   a) They will listen to you. Trust me!
   b) Stephen is going to the sea on Friday.
   c) We will probably be thinking of them at the time.
   d) Maybe they will do those reports tomorrow.
   e) What are they going to do over the weekend? They are going to ride their bikes.
   f) The exam is on Wednesday morning. – I will be there.
   g) I decide she will come with us and that's it.
   h) He has gone out. He is going to play football with his friends.
   i) The train will arrive on time, believe me.
   j) I think she won't recover too soon.

2.
   a) She will probably come later so don't wait for her.
   b) He is going to go out of the house soon, so come fast.
   c) He is going to buy a bike next week. He is going to ride it to school.
   d) What can I do now? I know! I'll read a book.
   e) I've planned to go on a vacation. I'm going to leave next week.
   f) It is going to snow tomorrow so put something warmer on.

g) I'll come to you next week if you want.

h) They are going to talk about that incident when they meet.

i) I've listened to the radio and find out about that show. I'm going to see it.

j) Hurry up! The train is going to leave.

3.

a) Mary <u>will come</u> home when her husband <u>calls</u> her.

b) They <u>will be cleaning</u> the house while the girls <u>are cooking</u>.

c) Please, wait quietly until he <u>calls</u> you in.

d) I <u>will be leaving</u> for the sea at noon tomorrow.

e) I hope she <u>will come</u> soon.

f) They have planned to go there. They <u>are going to leave</u> tomorrow.

g) What <u>will you be doing</u> in ten years' time?

h) After they <u>give</u> us the information, we <u>will go</u> there.

i) Stop doing that! <u>I'll punish you</u> you otherwise.

j) She <u>will come</u> with us as soon as she <u>has heard</u> we've booked the tickets.

English Grammar Practice

4.
- a) You'll leave there 10) after the bus comes.
- b) In a few moments 4) he'll have finished his test.
- c) We'll start working on this project 1) as soon as the committee has agreed with the plan.
- d) I'll tell that to my mother 3) when she comes back from work.
- e) Go and buy tickets 8) as soon as you have finished here.
- f) Kelly will cook dinner 7) after she washes her hands.
- g) Next week at this time 9) we'll be swimming in the ocean.
- h) When I see him, 6) I'll ask him to phone you.
- i) In ten years, 2) she'll have retired from work
- j) He said 5) he could come next week

5.
- a) Shall we <u>go</u> to the beach?
- b) She hopes she'll <u>be</u> back soon.
- c) They are going <u>to write</u> the report in the afternoon.
- d) Will you <u>cook</u> for me tonight.
- e) She is going <u>to attend</u> that course.
- f) Shall we <u>buy</u> tickets for the theatre?
- g) They won't <u>be</u> late.
- h) Shall I <u>do</u> that for you?
- i) I think I will <u>drink</u> some coffee.

English Grammar Practice
j) Will you <u>open</u> the door for me, please?

6.
    a) By the time I come back, they will have left.
    b) After he checks the report, he will change his mind, you'll see.
    c) They won't come back until you call them.
    d) Will he be lying in bed at this hour tomorrow?
    e) When the child comes back, I'll call you back.
    f) As soon as we have finished our work in the house, we will call on you.
    g) I'll see Mary tomorrow so I can tell her about your party.
    h) After the lecture ends, they will be going to the theatre.
    i) He will have gone to bed by the time you arrive.
    j) Alice will go to work by car after she has her car repaired.

7.

a) My son will go out to play when he has done his homework.

b) As soon as she has finished her work today, Sidney will manage to come to us.

c) What will she be working in ten years' time?

d) Mary is going to buy herself a new raincoat.

e) They are going to invite their friends to their party next Sunday.

f) Shall we have a cheese sandwich?

English Grammar Practice

g) Mary, will you help me here?

h) Please, John, don't go away before I come back.

i) They won't help me with my essay.

j) I won't be late.

8.
- a) Marian <u>is going to leave</u> next month.
- b) She <u>will be playing</u> the match of her life at ten tomorrow.
- c) They <u>will probably break</u> up soon.
- d) I expect they <u>will win</u> in this confrontation.
- e) She thinks they <u>will come</u> by train tomorrow.
- f) <u>Will he be working</u> at noon tomorrow? I want to call him.
- g) He <u>is just about to leave</u> so hurry up if you <u>want</u> to see him.
- h) She thinks she can't work here anymore so she <u>is about to resign</u>.
- i) The train <u>is due to leave</u> at nine.
- j) He <u>won't have won</u>, I suppose. The contest must have been very difficult.

UNIT 16: FUTURE – PROGRESS TEST

1.

   a) There's someone at the back door. – That will be Mary. She usually comes at the back door.

   b) We won't be late. The journey won't take more than two hours.

   c) Is he going to work next week? I want to invite him with us at the cottage.

   d) Don't come so late! I usually sleep at the hour.

   e) By the time she comes, I will have left.

   f) They have already packed. They are going to take the train very early in the morning.

   g) By tonight, you will decide, won't you?

   h) She has put the tomatoes in the pan. What is she going to do next?

   i) Please, call me as soon as you have found out the result of the test.

   j) By this time next month, they will have arrived in town.

English Grammar Practice

2.

a) The train will be late even though 2. it's due at ten

b) According to the radio forecast 1. it will rain tomorrow

c) Hurry if you want to see Alice because 3. she's about to leave

d) I'll decide what I do after 2. I see him

e) Mary will have written to him by the time 3. he comes back

f) In three months' time 1. he'll be living here

g) Don't wait for him because 1. he won't come

h) By the time Don arrives 1. we'll have finished everything

i) In two weeks, 2. I'll be working here

j) As soon as I have got their answer, 1. I'll let you know

3.
- a) As soon as he has seen his new house, he will write to us about it.
- b) Is he going to do anything on Friday evening? I have tickets for that rock concert.
- c) Wait for her until she's finished her assignments if you want to go out with her.
- d) When she is sixty, she will retire and move to the countryside to live there.
- e) I've lost my wallet! How am I going to buy a train ticket now?
- f) They are going to go to bed. You can't call them now.
- g) She won't be long. She is taking her hat.
- h) Don't worry, I will be in touch with them next week.
- i) You can call me then. I will be listening to the news at the hour.
- j) She will be mad, if you call and ask.

English Grammar Practice

4.

a) He won't have arrived in town.

b) The President thinks his party will win.

c) In two years' time at least, we'll have built this house.

d) By the end of the year, I will have been learning French for ten years.

e) By the time we come he won't have arrived.

f) A concert will take place in town tomorrow evening.

g) As soon as I have finished reading it, I'll give you the book back.

h) What do you think about going to the theatre tomorrow?

i) In two years I will have completed this project.

j) As soon as she's finished her work at the office, Sheila will probably come.

5.
- a) Andrew's sister will have left <u>by the time</u> we arrive.
- b) They will be having a meeting <u>at noon</u> tomorrow.
- c) There will not tests given <u>from now on</u>.
- d) Mathias and I will come <u>at noon</u>, I promise.
- e) She'll be teaching <u>soon</u>.
- f) They won't have written to us <u>in a week.</u>
- g) We are going to leave <u>at the end of the week</u>.
- h) I'll be back <u>when</u> the film starts.
- i) I can't come to you on Friday. I won't have finished everything <u>until then</u>.
- j) She'll be at home <u>in a few minutes</u>.

6.
   a) She won't be late.
   b) They are about to break relations with their neighbours.
   c) No one knows what she is going to do.
   d) They are taking their exams next month.
   e) She won't have finished her domestic works until I come.
   f) Who will give you a hand with your problem?
   g) Tell her that she will see me in front of the post office when she comes.
   h) What are you going to do over the weekend?
   i) John will call you up after he finishes his projects.
   j) Theodore is on the verge of making a big mistake.

UNIT 18: PRACTICE CONDITIONAL TYPE 1 AND 2

1.
- a) If they go there with us, they will see that I was right.
- b) If the rain stops, we'll go for a walk.
- c) I'll check the documents and if they are, I will join your business.
- d) If the wind blows, we won't be able to climb up that hill.
- e) If he tells, then we will be in a serious trouble.
- f) If they arrive, they will see the movie with us.
- g) If you read this novel, you will discover an interesting view on life.
- h) I hope he won't do it again. If he breaks the window again, Mr. Thompson will get angry.
- i) If they keep working like that, they will reach bankruptcy, to be sure.
- j) He will come to visit you tomorrow, if you give him a phone call and invite him.

English Grammar Practice

2.

a) I'm not sure when I have told them to come to the cinema. What shall I do? – Don't worry, if they come earlier, they will wait for us.

b) You say to a friend: An exhibition has just opened downtown. What do you say? Will you come with me? Your friend replies: If you invite me to come, I will join you.

c) Oh, John, we are in a real trouble. Can you help us? – Don't worry, if I can do something, I will do it.

d) You meet a friend you haven't seen for a long time and you say: If you want, I will invite you to my house on Sunday evening.

e) This is a very interesting painting exhibition. If you don't go to see it, you will regret.

f) You are with friends and find out that you have taken your exams. You say: Will you excuse me if I go to send a telegram to my parents about my exams?

g) A friend tells you that he doesn't know what happened with some common friends. You reply: Don't worry, if I talk to them, they will tell me everything.

h) I want to ask Mark to help me with this problem. If he does me this favour, I will be grateful to him.

i) I can't work out the answer. Who can help me? – What will you say if I tell you that I know the answer?

English Grammar Practice

j) I need your help in this matter. Will you help me if I ask you?

3.
a) We will go to a picnic tomorrow unless it rains.
b) She would agree with you if you told her the truth.
c) I would build a house in town if I had the money.
d) She won't come to you unless you invite her.
e) They would visit the Browns if they were invited.
f) She will go to hospital unless she recovers.
g) No one of his brothers could take care of him if he got sick.
h) My brother would never forgive me if I spoke to his boss.
i) He would be calmer if he knew that he was right.
j) You would think like me if you knew the entire story.

English Grammar Practice

4.

a) If you cared of your aunt, 4) you wouldn't treat her with so lack of respect.

b) If I were sure I didn't bother you, 8) I would tell you all the adventures we had during the summer holiday.

c) His brother would laugh at me 1) if he saw what I was doing

d) If your mother heard that, 9) what would she say?

e) If I told you what I saw in their office a few days ago 2) you wouldn't believe me.

f) I couldn't add anything more 6) if I were to make the presentation.

g) If she talked to him about that, 10) he would pretend he hadn't heard.

h) If someone saw her doing that stupid thing, 5) she would be very upset.

i) I would be against your projects 3) if I could have a word to say.

j) What would you do 7) if you had to make such a difficult decision?

5.
- a) I <u>would spend</u> a few days with you if I <u>had</u> money.
- b) I suppose he <u>will conclude</u> a contract with you if he <u>reads</u> your project.
- c) They <u>will go</u> swimming unless it <u>is</u>.
- d) If he <u>told</u> you about his trip, you <u>wouldn't believe</u> him.
- e) I couldn't interfere between them even though I <u>wanted</u>.
- f) He <u>would be</u> very disappointed if you <u>told</u> him the truth.
- g) If I <u>told</u> him what I heard, our friendship <u>would break</u>.
- h) Paul <u>would be forced</u> to resign if his boss <u>found out</u> the truth about him.
- i) If he <u>wants</u> to marry her, he must tell her too.
- j) If you <u>knew</u> the truth about her, you <u>wouldn't want</u> to be in touch with her anymore.

UNIT 19: PRACTICE CONDITIONAL TYPE 2 AND 3

1.

   a) She would have been surprised if she had heard that story. She couldn't have believed her eyes.

   b) I would have punished you for these words if I had been your mother.

   c) They would have left in due time if they had woken up early the other day.

   d) Shirley would have come to visit you if you had invited her, to be sure.

   e) If you told that to Peter, he would be very happy, you know.

   f) I suppose he would have eaten if you had told him that Mary was the cook. He likes her cooking. It's a pity you didn't do it!

   g) Do you think they would have done it if they had seen the plans? Then, why didn't you show them the plans?

   h) Don't be silly! Of course I would do it if I had time.

   i) You know, if I had had time, I would have taken driving lessons. Maybe next month I'll find the time.

   j) She didn't come! – Yes, I know. If she had had the means, she would have come.

English Grammar Practice

2.

a) What would you do if you could drive?

b) If I were you, I would try it.

c) If I were her, I would learn more.

d) If I were you, I would practice more.

e) If I were you, I would call him if he has problems.

f) If you did that, what would Ellen say?

g) If I were you, I'd change my behaviour.

h) If I were in your place I'd go there see with my own eyes.

i) If it rains tomorrow, I'll take the car.

j) How would you feel if she brought you the gift you expected?

3.
- a) If I <u>dared</u>, I <u>would address</u> you this question. Would you answer me?
- b) I <u>would have understood</u> better his deeds if I I <u>had known</u> the circumstances, but he didn't tell me anything.
- c) If I <u>weren't</u> too tired, I <u>would show you off</u>, but I want to go to bed now.
- d) I <u>would have spent</u> a few days with them if I <u>had had</u> vacation but unfortunately, I had to go to work.
- e) Your students <u>would have been</u> very amazed if you <u>had told</u> them about your research. You haven't told them so far, have you?
- f) She <u>wouldn't have gone</u> there if she <u>hadn't heard</u> that he was going to be there. That's why she came.

English Grammar Practice

g) Marilee <u>wouldn't have left</u> there hadn't she got their invitation.

h) <u>I I wouldn't have bought</u> bread if I <u>had known</u> that you also bought some.

i) Maria <u>would have written</u> to you if she <u>had known</u> your address but she asked me about it only a few days ago.

j) The boy <u>wouldn't go swimming</u> / if his mother <u>didn't allow</u> him to go, but she did.

English Grammar Practice

4.

a) If I had woken up early, I would have been at school in time.

b) If Mary had bought tickets in due time she could have gone to the show.

c) If Alice and I had left earlier, we would have managed to get there on time.

d) Had they bought something to eat in their way home, they could have cooked dinner .

e) Had Alice done her homework, she wouldn't have got a bad mark.

f) If we could leave early, we could get to the airport on time.

g) If she had caught the last bus, Maria wouldn't have had to take a cab.

h) Had Alison and John agreed with that matter, they wouldn't have broken up.

i) Had you eat something, you wouldn't feel so unwell.

j) Hadn't the boys fought in the schoolyard, they wouldn't have been punished.

5.

a) This is a good play. You would like it if you saw it.

b) If you had asked me to come with you, I would have refused you, and you know it.

c) I doubt he would feel the same about her if she told him her secret.

d) What would they have believed about me if I had done it?

e) Your father would have got mad if he had heard what you did.

f) Would you do it if you were asked to do it one day?

g) If Ann asked you to give her these books for a while, would you do it?

h) If she had asked him to help her with her suitcases, would he have done it?

i) If you had some spare time, what would you do?

j) He wouldn't be in this situation if he had listened to his father's advice, but he hadn't.

UNIT 20: PRACTICE WISHES

1.
- a) I wish I <u>spent</u> a few days in the mountains. I'm too tired.
- b) He wished he <u>had</u> a house in this neighbourhood. It is very quiet.
- c) She wishes she <u>had left</u> early. She wouldn't have been late.
- d) They wish they <u>could manage</u> but they couldn't.
- e) I wished I <u>had lived</u> in the country. It would have been more peaceful.
- f) They boy wishes he <u>had</u> such a toy car but he doesn't.
- g) She wishes she <u>had learnt</u> more because now she'd have been at the university.
- h) My aunt wished she <u>had gone</u> to France last year but she had no money.
- i) Lauren wishes she <u>bought</u> a car. Maybe next year she'll have the money.
- j) The teachers wish their students <u>studied</u> more but they don't do it.

2.

a) I am very tired and I'd like to go to bed but I haven't finished my homework. - 2. I wish I could go to bed.

b) She is very upset because of her son. - 1. She wishes he learnt more.

c) I left too late for work yesterday and I got into big trouble. - 2. I wish I had left earlier.

d) The woman is very sick now and she can't do anything. - 2. She wishes she had gone to the doctor sooner.

e) The little boy lost his toys yesterday and now he regrets. - 2. He wishes he had been more attentive.

f) The man was too tired and therefore he made an accident. -2. Now he wishes he hadn't driven and he had stayed at home.

g) She did very poor in her test yesterday. 2. She wishes she had studied more.

h) Alice is heartbroken now. -2. She wishes she hadn't broken up with David.

i) Edward and John went to the movies yesterday and missed Ann's visit. -2. They wish they had stayed home instead.

j) We missed the train in the morning and we had to wait for the next one. -2. We wish we hadn't wasted so much time at breakfast.

3.

   a) I'm thirsty. If only I had a bottle of mineral water.
   b) She is too tired. If only she had slept more last night.
   c) She is too fat now. If only she hadn't eaten so much.
   d) They are very sad now. If only they hadn't had a row because of that stupid thing and broken up. Now they would have still been together.
   e) She wishes she hadn't bought that dress. It was a waste of money.
   f) The teacher wishes he hadn't organized the trip to the mountain because his students did a lot of stupid things.
   g) If only I had had the answer to his question. Maybe I would have solved the entire situation.
   h) If only maths weren't so difficult. Maybe I would have better marks.
   i) He hopes he will do better in his next test. This one was a real mess.
   j) She hopes he will come tomorrow. She really needs his help.

4.

    a) I wish I had had more time to work on this project but I didn't have enough time.

    b) She wishes she went to the mountains soon.

    c) We wished we had met them when we were in Berlin.

    d) John wishes he had a new car.

    e) They wish they had been there last year too.

    f) Donna and Trish wish they had taken a cab but they hadn't.

    g) Lauren and I wish we visited them but we don't have the time.

    h) They wish she had come to their party but she left somewhere else.

    i) They wished I had lent them the book but I needed it too.

    j) I wished I had gone to that play. I hear it is great.

English Grammar Practice

UNIT 21: CONDITIONALS AND WISHES CONSOLIDATION

1.

a) If you had enough time, what would you do?

b) What would you take with you if you could go there?

c) If I were you, I'd do my work.

d) What would you say if they had been willing to come?

e) What would you put the robot to do if you had one?

f) If you could buy a trip to Paris, what would you say?

g) If I were you, I'd buy myself a dog.

h) If you could solve all their problems, what would you do?

i) If you were in his shoes, what would you do?

j) If someone told you the same things to you, how would you feel?

2.

    a) If I <u>were</u> you, I <u>would go</u> to the beach.

    b) If they <u>had had</u> time, they <u>would have gone</u> to the amusements park, but they hadn't.

    c) Unless it <u>rains</u>, I <u>will go</u> to the mountains with my friends.

    d) I <u>would have bought</u> a bike if I <u>had had</u> money, but I hadn't.

    e) The boy <u>wouldn't have been late</u> if he <u>had woken up</u> on time, but he woke up only at nine.

    f) You are not patient at all. If you <u>were</u>, you <u>might find out</u> / interesting things.

    g) If your son <u>had studied more</u>, he <u>could have been admitted</u> in the university.

    h) You are broke again. If you <u>hadn't spent</u> so much, you <u>might have had</u> some money left.

    i) <u>Hadn't he been</u> so distracted, he <u>might have noticed</u> she was actually looking and smiling at him.

    j) <u>Hadn't it been</u> for her, they <u>wouldn't have had</u> that chance.

3.

a) Had he bought tickets, we could have gone to the movie.

b) Hadn't she missed the train, she could have come with us.

c) Hadn't they lost their way, they would have reached the chalet.

d) Hadn't Shirley been upset with him, she would have gone to meet him.

e) Hadn't we been so lazy, we would have helped them.

f) Hadn't you left in a hurry, you would have seen her.

g) Hadn't I lost my purse in town, I could have bought something for dinner.

h) Hadn't she been absent-minded, she wouldn't have forgotten to buy some bread and milk.

i) Had I wanted to meet them, I wouldn't have told them I was out of town for a while.

j) But for Mark's help, I wouldn't have succeeded in my project.

English Grammar Practice

4.

a) I'm hungry now. I wish <u>had eaten</u> in the morning.

b) I'm not well. I wish I <u>hadn't drunk</u> so much syrup.

c) If only I <u>had had</u> a car. I could be there in time.

d) If only I <u>hadn't read</u> so much! I have a migraine.

e) I hope <u>I will come</u> to your anniversary.

f) I wish you <u>saw</u> that. It's fantastic!

g) I wish I <u>had had</u> a bigger house. I could have friends over.

h) But for them, she <u>wouldn't have come</u>.

i) Supposing they had a boat, we <u>could have sailed</u> in the Caribbean.

j) She wished she <u>hadn't sent that letter</u>.

5.

    a) I'm very tired. I wish I had a rest.

    b) It is lovely here. I wish I had a house here.

    c) My stomach hurts. I wish hadn't eaten that sandwich.

    d) It seems to be a lovely place. I hope I'll spend a lot of time here.

    e) If only it hadn't rained so much. I've forgotten my umbrella and I'm wet.

    f) This purse is a real piece of work. I wish I had had money to buy it.

    g) They want to go there soon. If only they had a few days off!

    h) If only had money on me! That's a beautiful coat.

    i) I have a terrible headache! If only my neighbours had stopped the noise!

    j) But for her intervention, he wouldn't have got the contract.

UNIT 23: PRACTICE MODAL VERBS

1.
- a) I think he <u>might</u> come tomorrow.
- b) You <u>had better</u> leave soon. They're waiting.
- c) You <u>should</u> do your homework.
- d) That's not right. This <u>can't</u> be the answer.
- e) It's ringing at the door. It <u>must</u> be John.
- f) They left half an hour ago. They <u>must</u> be there now.
- g) I <u>can't</u> go out. I have some work to do.
- h) You <u>must</u> write it down. You'll forget it.
- i) You are crazy. You <u>shouldn't</u> eat too much.
- j) Ann <u>must</u> be home now. She finishes work at five.

2.

a) John might come to your party.

b) We have to do our homework because we have a very severe teacher and we get bad marks otherwise.

c) They are in town now, but they might come back at noon.

d) You shouldn't eat so much because you will have stomach ache.

e) Jill can't come to you because she's sick.

f) He must do the work very well as he knows a lot about this subject.

g) She may not go to the beach today because she's grounded.

English Grammar Practice

h) You'd better not stay in the sun because it is too bright and you'll get sunburnt.

i) The child must be sleeping now because he has played a lot.

j) You needn't do that too.

3.
- a) Alice might move out soon.
- b) You shouldn't drink so much beer.
- c) I think he must have come home.
- d) I've heard a car stopping in front of the house but it can't be them as they don't have a car.
- e) Smoking is bad for you. You had better give up smoking and you will feel better.
- f) I ought to leave because I'll be late for work.
- g) You needn't write everything.
- h) It may rain tomorrow.
- i) The meeting starts at ten and you can't be late.
- j) I must go home because I have work to do.

4.

a) You shouldn't go there. You'll have a lot of trouble.
b) Children mustn't go out without their parents.
c) He must learn this time because otherwise he'll fail again.
d) You had better hurry. The bus will leave without you.
e) He must be here at midnight. – Yes, I think so.
f) I shouldn't have done that stupid thing!
g) When he was a child, he didn't have to do so much work.
h) You must have forgotten it at home.
i) I think she must have taken the train instead.
j) She must have sung well when she was younger.

5.

a) When I was at school, I had to learn a lot.
b) Oh, dear! What an idea! You could have fallen!
c) They didn't come yesterday. They might have not finished their work. (
d) You're completely run down. You shouldn't have worked so hard.
e) She can't find her book. She must have lost it.
f) I couldn't talk to him because the line was busy.
g) They might have failed in the exam because they didn't pay enough attention in class.
h) She graduated the first. She must have worked hard.

English Grammar Practice
i) I needn't have helped them with their furniture because they could have managed by themselves.

j) He thinks that he might left it at home.

English Grammar Practice

UNIT 25: PRACTICE PASSIVE VOICE

1.

    a) The boy was taught English at school <u>by a teacher</u>.

    b) The car was stolen <u>by someone</u> yesterday.

    c) He was fined in the street <u>by a policeman</u>.

    d) The meat was stolen <u>by the cat</u>.

    e) He was put some questions <u>by someone</u>.

    f) The fish was caught <u>by a man</u>.

    g) They were told to the teacher <u>by their colleagues</u>.

    h) The sink was fixed <u>by a plumber</u>.

    i) The car was bought <u>by someone</u>.

    j) She was injured <u>by someone</u> yesterday.

2.

a) He was asked about the new rules.

b) Her purse was left on the desk.

c) New bags were bought from that shop.

d) The garden was dug in the morning.

e) The great poem "The Morning Star" was written by Eminescu.

f) America was discovered by Columbus.

g) A part of Africa was colonised by British.

h) Napoleon was defeated during his campaign in the East by Russians.

i) Cats are chased by dogs.

j) Earth is warmed up by the Sun.

English Grammar Practice

3.
- a) Nothing was decided then.
- b) They were hit by a car.
- c) She sewed her dress with a needle.
- d) We were lost in the woods.
- e) Houses are being built in the neighbourhood now.
- f) The students were being examined when I came in.
- g) The lights had been turned off when I got there.
- h) The dog will be taken to a walk at noon.
- i) The work will be done by then.
- j) The wild animals in the zoo will be fed soon.

4.
- a) We are having our house painted tomorrow.
- b) She has had her hair cut.
- c) We had our car mended yesterday.
- d) You have had your furniture brought.
- e) She had her purse stolen.
- f) She had her window broken the other day.
- g) I had my washing machine repaired in the morning.
- h) Tomorrow, I will have my child taken from school.
- i) They'll have their exams corrected tomorrow.
- j) By noon tomorrow, I will have had my kitchen refurnished

English Grammar Practice

5.

a) He became member of the committee last year.

b) The person behind her asked her if she was getting off at the next bus stop.

c) Their boss requested that they do their projects.

d) Her mother told her to go there.

e) They appointed me head of department last year.

f) Some famous authors wrote these books.

g) Her mother left her a note to ask her to do the plans for the vacation.

h) The housekeeper arranged the toys in the child's room.

i) Someone came and left me a note.

j) No one present at the meeting yesterday believed him.

6.

    a) They were told some awful stories and they are still scared.

    b) He was asked a difficult question but he couldn't answer.

    c) Mary asked her son to do that job and he did what he was told.

    d) The report was completed two days ago.

    e) Someone told her to go there and she went where she was told to go.

    f) Someone left you a package with the receptionist.

    g) The bridge was built a few years ago.

    h) She thinks you are right because she was shown some evidence.

    i) The garbage was taken outside an hour ago. Janine did it.

    j) They were required to answer to all the questions on the paper.

UNIT 27: PRACTICE REPORTED SPEECH

1.

a) John told me he was coming to me.

b) The students said they wanted a break.

c) Mary told me that Dan had just left.

d) She said that the cat had eaten an hour ago.

e) Luke's mother told me he hadn't passed his exam.

f) Mary told us that they would be back soon.

g) Her sister told him that Mary was sleeping at that moment.

h) John said that it would rain the next day.

i) I said that we would be late and we'd better hurry.

j) She said with anger that he had lost it.

2.

a) "I've missed the train", she said.

b) "The car is broken", we told them.

c) "Why have you missed your classes today", mother asked them.

d) "I've slept till late", John told us.

e) "We won't come with you", Sean and Andrew said.

f) "Have you bought me a toy?" the child asked.

g) "We've arrived on time", they said on the phone.

h) "I'm going to leave soon", Sheila told me.

i) "We've written a note for you", they said.

j) "I'll be there on time", you told me.

English Grammar Practice

3.
  a) She told me that she would come next day.
  b) They told us that they had done their homework already.
  c) Melanie said that she was ill.
  d) Mother and father told us that they would come back at three.
  e) Lucy and Dan said that they had been dancing all night the other day.
  f) Betty and I told them that we had written two letters to Aunt Alice by then.
  g) He said that he was going to leave the town.
  h) You told them that you had led John to the airport.
  i) The boy told his mother that his class was going to take a trip to Manchester.
  j) We told to the teacher that we were just writing the essay.

4.
  a) Mother asked John to go to the store.
  b) We invited Mary to come to us on Friday.
  c) Mother called us to dinner.
  d) The professor sent the student back to his seat.
  e) I asked him to stop asking silly questions.
  f) Angrily, he asked me to leave that thing on the table and get out.
  g) Mark requested her to stop saying that all the time.
  h) I advised them to take the bus from the corner of that street.

English Grammar Practice

    i) The man advised the tourists to go and visit the castle.

    j) Mother asked the children not to ask so many questions.

5.

    a) She told me that I had to go there in the afternoon.

    b) We advised them not to take tickets to that show.

    c) I wanted to have a black coffee and I said that.

    d) John congratulated Ann because she had passed her exam.

    e) William promised to come with us.

    f) John asked the librarian to give him that book.

    g) He promised to bring them the tapes.

    h) They apologized because they had made such a blunder.

    i) We agreed with their idea.

    j) She promised to come earlier that day.

6.

    a) John advised Ann not to go there.

    b) I invited them to the cinema that evening.

    c) The boy offered to take my bag.

    d) Alice proposed to give it to me.

    e) George refused to do it.

    f) He agreed with my idea.

    g) Mother congratulated Alice for having taken her driving license.

English Grammar Practice

    h) Mel apologised for being late.

    i) Stan reminded me to go there.

    j) The boy suggested that I'd join them for the party.

    k) They agreed to come to the festival.

    l) His colleague asked him the book for the day.

7.

    a) John asked me whether I had brought the tickets.

    b) They asked her if she would come with them.

    c) Peter asked Dan if he was staying at the hotel that summer.

    d) He asked me if I was going to take that day off.

    e) Alice asked them if they had been to Cambridge that week.

    f) Paul asked me if I was doing my work when he phoned me.

    g) Donna asked them if they would work with them the next day.

    h) Father asked Jill if she had spent a lot in town.

    i) Mother asked Alan if he was eating then.

    j) My cousin asked me if they had already got there.

English Grammar Practice

8.

a) I asked him when he had come back.

b) He asked her why she was so late.

c) He asked the boy what he was doing there.

d) She asked me where I had been.

e) I asked the baker how much it cost.

f) The little girl asked her brother how long he had been doing that.

g) I asked Ann when she was coming back.

h) I asked him where she lived.

i) Do you know when the shop closes?

j) Could you tell me the meaning of this thing?

Also by Roxana Nastase:

English Grammar Practice – The Noun:
Explanations & Exercises with Answers

English Grammar Practice

www.ingramcontent.com/pod-product-compliance
Lightning Source LLC
Chambersburg PA
CBHW081438070526
44586CB00019B/2170